# A LOOK AT
# WHITE IRONSTONE

With Text and Drawings
by

JEAN WETHERBEE

Copyright © 1980
Jean Wetherbee

ISBN 0-87069-293-3

Library of Congress
Catalog No. 79-64961

Second Printing, 1981

Photograph: Wheat patterned white ironstone
by Perry Struse, West Des Moines, Iowa.

Published by

**Wallace-Homestead Book Company**
1912 Grand Avenue
Des Moines, Iowa 50309

To
    Linda whose confidence and
    enthusiasm kept me
    going and . . .

To
    Doris whose tireless search
    for information kept
    me compiling.

*Plain white ironstone is attractively arranged on pumpkin pine table. Surplus pieces are stored in old pine jelly cupboard. Photograph: LeBel.*

# Contents

|       | Acknowledgments | 6 |
|-------|-----------------|---|
| I     | Getting Started | 7 |
| II    | Before White Ironstone | 10 |
| III   | One Hundred Years of Ironstone | 18 |
| IV    | On the Underside | 20 |
| V     | The Process of Potting | 31 |
| VI    | What's in a Set? | 33 |
| VII   | Earliest White Ironstone | 37 |
| VIII  | Sydenham and Similar Shapes | 48 |
| IX    | Famous Names | 59 |
| X     | Golden Waves of Grain | 69 |
| XI    | Green of the Earth | 78 |
| XII   | Flower Garden | 91 |
| XIII  | Ribs and Revival | 103 |
| XIV   | Patterns of the Seventies and Eighties | 109 |
| XV    | After 1891 | 120 |
| XVI   | Copper Tea Leaf Ironstone | 122 |
| XVII  | Relish Dishes | 126 |
| XVIII | Native White Ironstone | 133 |
| XIX   | Is It Worth Keeping? | 141 |
| XX    | Fun with Ironstone | 145 |
| XXI   | In Conclusion | 151 |
|       | Bibliography | 153 |
|       | Index | 155 |
|       | About the Author | 159 |

## Acknowledgments

I am grateful for the help and encouragement so freely given by the following individuals and groups listed here:

My friends and neighbors who gave and lent me their pieces to copy: the Nasses, the Kuligs, the Pecoras, the Van Wies, the Russos, the Dollards, the Knudsens, the Dingmans, the Dalenbergs, the Flanigans, and others.

The collectors who shared their knowledge and let me study their treasures: John and Beverly Black, James and Doris Walker, Carol and Gary Grove, John and Jane Yunginger, Mr. and Mrs. William Horner, Kenneth and Alice Johnson, Jane Diemer, John and Lois Rhines, Shirley Montgomery, Charles and Harriet Hoover, Sarah Province, Mr. and Mrs. Thomas Richardson, Mrs. Dawson Farber, Jean Hogg, the Zerns, and many others.

Those responsive readers of my first handbook who wrote me about their collections, sent drawings and snapshots, or just urged me to keep searching for more information.

The many antique dealers who were interested enough to let me explore on and under their shelves and to those who lent me their white ironstone: McGregor's Antiques, Exit 29 Antiques, Tom Needham's Shop, the Vermont shop of Dr. and Mrs. Stuart Orton, and several others.

Saltsman's Hotel in Ephratah, New York, who allowed us to photograph their beautiful tureens.

The individual collectors who contributed photographs for use in this book, LeBel Studios, John Black, and especially Clarke Blair, who used much creative skill as he worked with white ironstone.

Lois Bunce who typed and retyped this text patiently and well.

# I  Getting Started

I can still hear my mother direct, "Go down cellar and get some dill pickles before the men come in from the field." Down I would go to the cool cellar, stoop beside a four gallon crock, lift out the large round "pickle stone," tip up a heavy octagon-shaped white plate, push aside the protective grape leaves and fish out enough dill pickles for dinner. The serving dish full, the whole order was reversed with the stone banging and grating against the sturdy dish as it sank down in the brine. That old plate was really tough!

Next to that pickle crock, another smaller crock kept preserves which were weighted down by a smaller white plate decorated with ears of corn and stalks of oats in relief.

Outside the kitchen door of that farmhouse built in the Mohawk Valley of New York State, a pine wash bench was readied for the tired grimy men. I gathered a blue enameled dipper and wash basins to set on it; my brother lugged out a pail each of hot and cold water; another sister hung clean huck towels on the clothesline nearby. Conveniently resting between the blue basins, I can still see a boat-shaped white dish holding two cakes of home-made soap. The edge of the "soap dish" was impressed with wheat heads and blades. Deep down inside were scallops.

When the pickles and preserves were gone, those two white plates were brought upstairs and used whenever we needed a sturdy, expendable dish. They covered the crocks of newly-tried lard; they gathered table scraps; they held the fare for the family shepherd dog. That oval dish spent the winter in the back shed filled with rusty wire scrapers and the ends of soap cakes.

These are my earliest recollections of the plain white ironstone that collectors are picking up today. I finally studied the diamond-shaped mark on the bottom of the octagon plate and was amazed to discover that that dish had been working for more than one hundred years. Anything else that old would have been tenderly displayed or at least collecting social security!

My curiosity grew. I studied those three dishes and those of friends who had a piece or two of "great-grandma's old white ironstone," as we called them. I located some beautifully preserved old chocolate pots, great soup tureens complete with ladle and cracker tray, graceful gravy boats, and occasionally a handleless cup with its deep saucer. Most of these heirlooms had a sort of bluish cast and many had a glaze that was unstained, free of age cracks and chips. I also found the possessors quite reluctant to part with these rarer pieces since most of them had been long in the family.

Years later, some of our rural neighbors, choosing to preserve the air of early-American country life, sensed that a row of heavy white plates along the top of a pine hutch or a graceful white pitcher filled with black-eyed susans added just the touch they desired. When they wanted to reinforce the simplicity of former days, homemakers polished up old wooden utensils and hung them in a row, waxed the old barrel churn, and noted that the startling accent of white ironstone completed the picture.

As happens to many collectors who become interested in a certain field, I began to dig for information about these plain dishes. I could find little real information. A few short articles by other collectors increased my interest and raised many more questions.

Why had no English collectors gathered the facts about the white ironstone their country had shipped to America by the thousands? If good pieces were snatched up so quickly at antique shops and taken home to warm a corner for an "antique lover," why was there no information available? All sorts of other books on pressed glass, cut-glass, wooden-ware, pottery, silver, tin-ware, advertising items and many other subjects were flooding the market to please specific collectors. Why nothing on white ironstone? The search was on.

After studying the history of the making of English china, I began to see the reason why the English were uninterested in making a record of ironstone. The skills of great pottery firms such as Wedgwood, Minton, Adams, Ridgway, Mason and many, many others were employed and constantly being improved to try to produce porcelain as decorative, as delicate and durable as that being imported from China. This creative art was a source of much pride to the English potters. Meanwhile, each pottery was engaged in a business that required good management. The potting of durable white wares which could be both cheaply produced and readily sold in the markets on the continent of Europe and in the United States helped to ease financial problems. However, the English potters had pride only in their finer wares.

The best-known of the English potters in the last quarter of the eighteenth century, Josiah Wedgwood, wrote about the general exporting of china: "Our consumption is very trifling in comparison to what is sent abroad . . . to the continent and the islands of North America. To the continent, meaning Europe, we send an amazing quantity of white stoneware and some of the finer kinds, but for the islands, meaning America, we cannot make anything too rich or costly."

Thus we perceive that this plain ware had no cultural or historical significance to English potters. In America, the story was different.

The early colonists were so busy wresting a living from the land, clearing their acres, and watching Indians, that except for the wealthy gentry, there was little time to be concerned with elegant table services. They used the wooden trenchers, pewter dishes if they could be secured, and the rough red ware not dissimilar to that used in our common flower pots today. The few potters labored diligently making bricks and tiles for construction and shaping the very necessary housewares that were too clumsy to import: pots, jugs, milk pans, crocks, etc. Wedgwood had noted that America was rich in all the resources necessary for the making of dishes. Especially during the periods when England and the colonies were waging wars, abortive attempts were made to produce simple tablewares but the American potteries did not flourish until the 1870s and 1880s. Perhaps, the average citizen of this new and untried land was so concerned with the hills and valleys that stretched beyond the western horizon that he had no time to examine or shape the clay at his feet.

Therefore, when the potters from the Staffordshire area of England began to offer less expensive wares, the American housewife was a hungry customer. Many of the blue and white dishes, simply labeled Staffordshire wares today, were imported and eagerly purchased during the first half of the nineteenth century. By the late 1830s the workers in English clay had perfected an even more inexpensive, durable, and plentiful type of earthenware dish. Even the poorest of rural families gladly put away their wooden trenchers and red ware to set their tables in spotless white.

It was doubtless in the hearts of many of these homes that the restless urge to go west originated. Here were the kind of dishes that could be packed easily and were tough enough to take trail life. One of our ancestors writes that from his home on the bank of the Mohawk River, the greatest break in the Appalachian Chain that stretches from Canada to Georgia, he could watch the covered wagons going up the valley "like ships under full sail." Somehow I think that loaded away with the water jugs, the rounded trunks, the homespun blankets, and the churn, there must often have been sturdy white ironstone.

In the new homes that were built along the way, homemakers were glad to urge their frugal husbands to use a little of their year's profit to buy a set of dishes. Today, by looking in the homes of the offspring we can piece together a picture of that first treasured set. And that is just what I have tried to do in this book.

First, I visited neighbors, then local antique shops, and finally collections all over the East. I found that approximately 200 shapes were made in white ironstone by Staffordshire potters south of Liverpool in England. Today, collectors are looking all over this great country for their favorite patterns. What stories these dishes could tell us about the growing American years!

After all this pondering, I've come to the conclusion that ironstone met a need and added pleasure to the period in our history when our country was expanding the fastest.

*This rare ironstone ladle with branch handle and spout on the side is accompanied by a knife sharpener with ironstone handle and an invalid feeder. All from the collection of Mr. and Mrs. John Black. Photograph: Black.*

*FLUTED PEARL plate and chamber pot filled with springerle fern complement pine paneling. Photograph: Blair.*

# II  Before White Ironstone

Nearly all of the English dishes we call ironstone now were produced in the Staffordshire area of England where materials were available and the port of Liverpool was a convenient distance to the north and west. Here lived colonies of proud, capable potters in the nine settlements of Tunstall, Longport, Burslem, Cobridge, Hanley, Stoke, Fenton, Longton, and Lane End. Doubtless other areas of England produced similar wares but we seldom come across them here in the states. Staffordshire men say, "Working in earth makes men easy-minded."

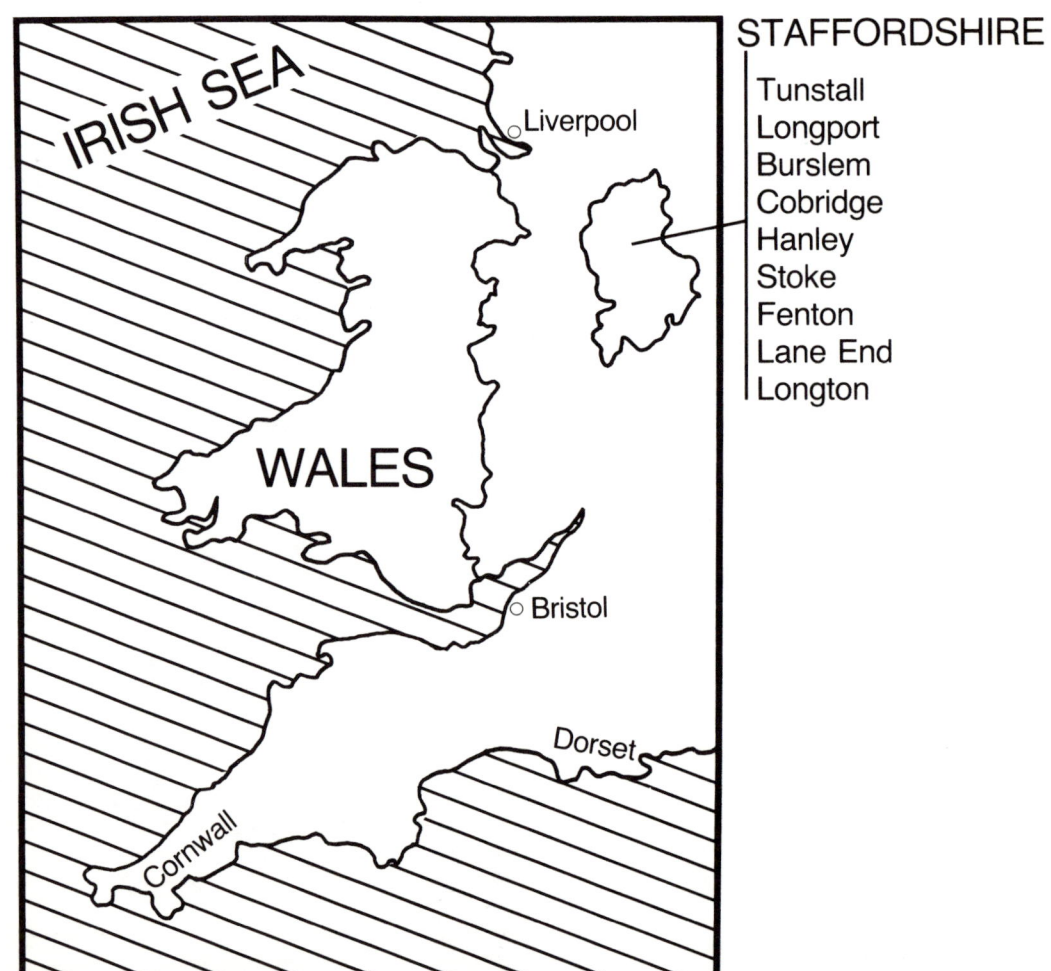

**Pottery Settlements**

The great Josiah Wedgwood, who centered his pottery in Staffordshire, never made the durable wares we know as ironstone, but he certainly had an influence that resulted in its later production. He was interested in many fields other than the business of pottery and aware of the forces at work in the countries and continents of the world. Wedgwood avidly followed the news that came back to England from her colonies across the wide Atlantic. A supporter of the causes of the American Revolution, he was still businessman enough to become concerned that his firm might lose its colonial market.

Eight or nine years before the war for independence began, Wedgwood sent a Mr. Griffith to South Carolina for white clay, a fine white earth called "Ayoree" by the natives. The Cherokee Indians there had been making excellent pipes from this clay for years. Mr. Griffith brought back five tons of this clay and it was found to be of fairly good quality. However, the Cornish clays were superior and could be had more simply and cheaply!

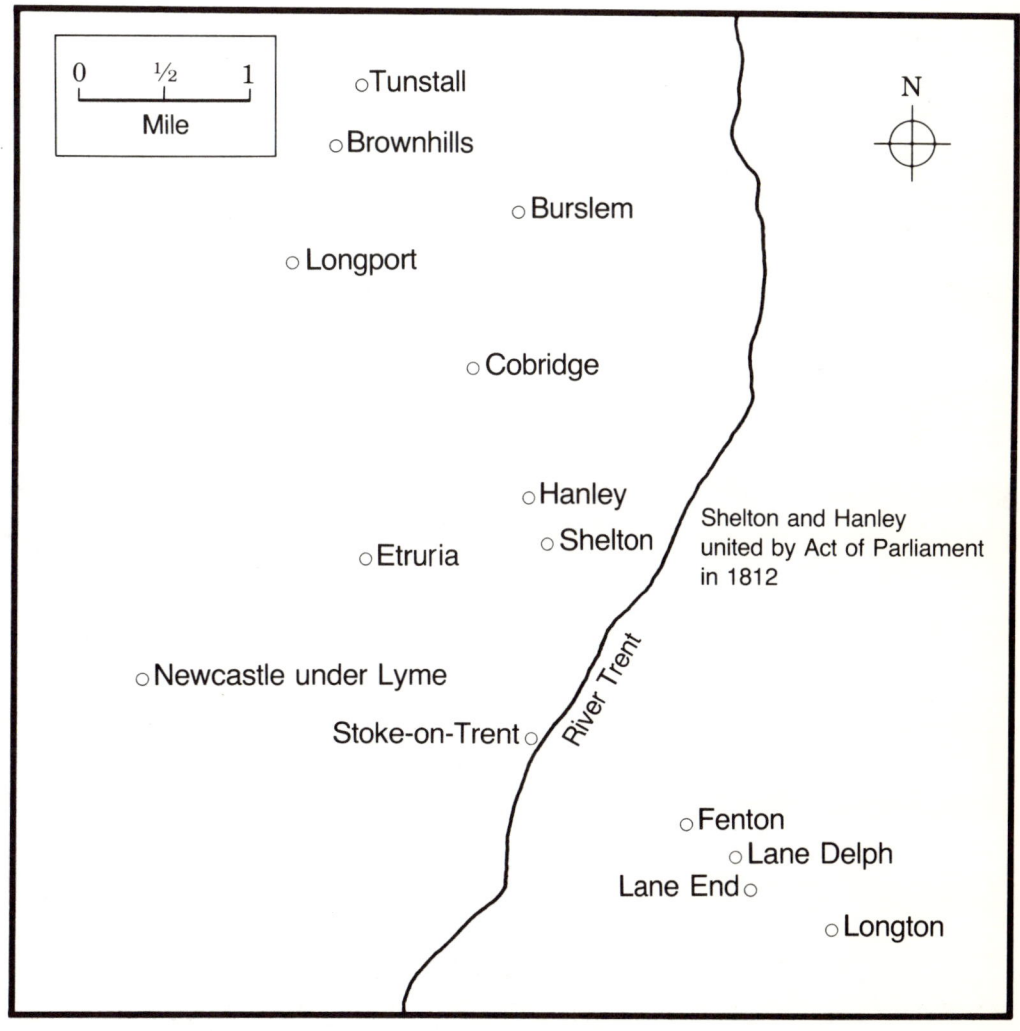

**Staffordshire Potteries 1800 A.D.**

The great potter occasionally continued to voice a fear that able English potters would go to America and be lost to the English industry. The Revolution kept the colonists so busy that no serious potteries were established. The white clays of the Cherokee lands were daubed with the blood of the battling colonists and the invading English. Meanwhile, the American housewives gladly drank their "liberty tea" from rough moulded redware cups. In reality, Wedgwood had little to fear as the American Revolution destroyed all competition.

Surprisingly, the war was scarcely over when trade with England flourished again. The English merchants were eager to supply the American markets, and the new country had a hankering for those goods that they had had no time to manufacture themselves.

In 1768, William Cookworthy had obtained an English patent that gave him the right for the sole use of *china clay* and *china stone* (see Chapter V). Richard Champion had taken over the patent in 1774, causing a group of Staffordshire potters headed by Josiah Wedgwood to rise up in protest a year later. Champion was granted the use of the materials to manufacture transparent ware only. This opened a whole new field, for after this any potter had the right to experiment with these materials in the potting of opaque china.

In 1784, Richard Champion, that able though controversial potter, left Bristol for North America and unsuccessfully experimented with the Cherokee clays there. He finally was attracted to the stretching acres, settled on a plantation nearby, became a planter and eventually filled several public offices. Thus, Wedgwood's fears of American rivalry were groundless.

Wedgwood had produced a cream-colored ware called "Queen's ware." Then, in 1779, he first made "pearlware." This was not made in great quantity but is important as a "precursor of the durable white granite wares made later by such potters as Maddock, Meakin, and Grindley," according to the account written by Graham and Wedgwood. This, of course, was a reference to the china bodies with which this book is concerned. The whiter body was invented by increasing the proportion of china clay and flint, and adding to the clay mixture a minute quantity of oxide of cobalt to neutralize the last traces of the yellow color. (We housewives understand this process since all of us have added bluing to whiten our washes.)

An interesting letter written by Wedgwood in 1787 to his friend, Bentley, attributes the discovery of the improvement in the white stoneware by the addition of calcined flint. He said:

> The *white stoneware* was produced by using the white pipe clay instead of the common clay of this neighborhood, and mixing it with flint stones calcined and reduced by pounding into a fine powder. The use of flint in our pottery is said to have proceeded from an accident happening to one of our potters, a Mr. Heath of Shelton, on his way to London. His horse's eye becoming bad, he applied to an hostler on the road, who told him he could cure the horse and showed him what means he used. Accordingly he took a piece of black flint stone and put it into the fire, which, to our potter's great astonishment, came out of the fire a most beautiful white, and at the same time struck him with an idea that this fine material might improve the stoneware lately introduced among them.
>
> He brought some of the stones home with him, mixed them with pipe clay and made the first *white flint stoneware*.

Other authors, however, claim that Dwight of Fulhams used calcined beaten and sifted flints in his wares fifty years earlier. Astbury is also claimed as inventor of this process.

Certainly, Josiah Wedgwood had a great influence on the pottery world because he was so supportive of new ideas, he was the originator of mass production, and he developed worldwide markets.

We cannot leave the name of Wedgwood without mentioning his talented relative, Ralph. His pottery was not successful; he was ruined financially through losses during the American War. His creative mind produced many new ideas, three of which were patented in 1796 and relate to the development of sturdy china. Firstly, he discovered a new, less costly method of "casing over inferior compositions commonly used for white ware." Secondly, he perfected a new glass-like finish by the addition of alkaline salts or borax to which was added calcareous earth, etc. His last contribution was an improved stove, a potter's oven with fireplaces situated within instead of on the outside, as had been usually done. Then, in the nineteenth century, he turned his efforts to inventing in other fields.

Two events occurred in the last decade of the eighteenth century which hastened the development of new kinds of opaque china. Champion's patent had finally expired in 1796, when the Cornish materials became accessible for any purpose that the potters required. In 1794, a high tariff had been imposed on imported porcelain. As results, the Chinese trade slowed down and the English potters initiated experiments with new bodies.

William and John Turner of Caughley were the first well-known potters to market an inexpensive durable type of earthenware that could compete with the popular imported Chinese ware. It was composed of "New Rock" Cornish stone and prepared flint. This firm became bankrupt in 1806.

Josiah Spode II, from Stoke-on-Trent, also manufactured a similar china. It was opaque with a far finer texture than previous earthenware; it emitted a clear ring when lightly tapped. Its dense body was so fine that it resembled porcelain. The body of Spode's original version of felspathic ware had a delicate blue-gray tint. This color was to be repeated in the later mass-produced "felspar china," another name for ironstone. Spode called this ware "Stone China" at first; later, it was marked "New Stone."

Other potters too, such as Davenport and Hicks & Meigh, marketed sets of china with a hard opaque body decorated gaily to imitate the Chinese imports. There was a vast world market begging for these useful stone wares.

Working with his sons, Miles Mason of Lane Delph mastered a very similar process. Then, in 1813, his son, Charles James Mason, made public his "Patent Ironstone China." Although his product was not much different from those of his competitors, the name appealed to the buyers. Mason was a good huckster and soon housewives on the continent and in America clamored for "ironstone" china. This new term became a permanent addition to the ceramic vocabulary.

Experts concede that the Rorstrand factory in Sweden was producing an admirable ironstone china or *flintporslin* as early as 1780. We must not fail to remember too that it was the excellent Chinese imports with their brilliant glazes and hard bodies that really prompted the English potters to innovate. They experimented in secret, produced their own special china bodies, and used good business practices to try to outsell their competitors. The abstract of Mason's July, 1813 patent read as follows:

> A process for the improvement of the manufacture of English porcelain, this consists of using the scoria or slag of Ironstone pounded and ground in water with certain proportions, with flint, Cornwall stone and clay, and blue oxide of cobalt.

Mason's patent was granted for a period of fourteen years and was not renewed, probably because the other major potters had perfected their own ironstone bodies by 1827. Godden in his book, *The Illustrated Guide to Mason's Patent Ironstone China,* writes that: "Several authorities have stated that the materials mentioned in the patent would not, on their own, make a workable ceramic body, and that the patent specification was a misleading front." At any rate, Mason has gone down in pottery history as introducing a durable, heavy earthenware called "Patent Ironstone China."

*1. Blue hexagonal jug, an example of Mason's early ironstone, a forerunner of the octagonal shapes that were to become so popular in white ironstone. Photograph: Blair.*

It may be interesting to the reader to know the firm names that have manufactured Mason wares through the years. Geoffrey Godden in his *Encyclopedia of British Pottery and Porcelain Marks* lists them as potters of "Mason's Ironstone":

| | |
|---|---|
| G.M. & C.J. Mason, | c. 1813 – 1829 |
| Charles James Mason & Co., | c. 1829 – 1845 |
| Charles James Mason, | c. 1845 – 48 and 1851 – 54 |
| Francis Morley (& Co.) | c. 1848 – 1862 |
| G.L. Ashworth & Bros., | c. 1862 – |

Beginning about 1810, these newer and cheaper wares were decorated with underglaze blue printing. Our ancestors loved to buy "Historic Staffordshire" china that attempted to picture places and events dear to growing America. It has been said that the sale of these deep blue designs applied to white ironstone did more to heal the wounds caused by the War of 1812 than all the words of great British and American leaders. In the twenty-five years following the conflict, dish-hungry America was flooded with mass-produced ironstone china decorated with cobalt blue. Wealthy citizens still preferred porcelain but the blue and white earthenware was eagerly purchased by merchants and professionals. Soon these flow blue dishes lowered in price enough so that many householders from the lower classes were able to own a set. With the over-production, some shoddy, poor quality pottery was produced.

Many of the cobalt blue pieces were not marked but can be attributed to certain potters by noting the border designs, a sort of prideful trademark. We come across marked plates from two different firms with the same center scene or design. The shrewd potters blatantly borrowed scenes from each other but respected the borders as belonging only to the originator. W. Adams circled his plates with baskets of roses and medallions; Wood used shells in his borders; Stubbs mixed eagles, scrolls, and flowers on the edges of his earthenware.

E. Wood & Co. potted the earliest known English blue and white earthenware, and Ralph and James Clews manufactured exceptionally beautiful flow blue dishes from 1818 to 1838. (James came to the States in 1836 to venture unsuccessfully into the pottery business at Troy, Indiana.) Many authors have found the subject of these old blue dishes interesting and have written extensively about them. A few of the titles are listed at the end of this chapter in case you like to explore.

The old blue dishes were decorated by transfer methods. Designs were kept uniform by using a die which was coated with color. A thin paper was pressed on the coated design, removed, and then placed on the area to be decorated. There were about sixty-five known artists who depicted over seven hundred subjects. The rich, dark blue color is the most collectible today.

In the 1830s the potters began using other colors such as black, brown, green, red, pink, mulberry, and light blue. The purplish-brown mulberry and the light blue were employed most.

This lighter and duller tint of blue transfer Staffordshire was manufactured from the mid-thirties on into the fifties. The pattern name was usually printed on the back in a foliated or flowery cartouche; often, an oval or oblong wreath-type mark was used.

The white ironstone about which this book is concerned first appeared in the same shapes as the dishes decorated with light blue transfers. Those examples I have seen have been made from the same molds; one in plain white and the other overlaid with a design in blue transfer. I finally got two of them together to get their picture taken as shown in Photograph 2.

We have at last arrived at our favorite subject among dishes — white ironstone. From our discussions you will learn to recognize the typical English potter. He was aware of the tastes of his prospective customer; he was alert to notice the success of a new idea and often adapted it to enhance his own products. Strong pottery families handed their knowledge down through generations and were quite unwilling to publicize their new discoveries. Perhaps that is why a potter like Mason was willing to patent a name and a recipe listing the wrong proportions. These potters produced thousands and thousands of white ironstone sets before the century closed.

2. *Relish dishes formed from the same molds tell us that the transition from the transfer designs to the plain white designs was a gradual process. Many Gothic designs are found decorated or left plain, the latter practice becoming more popular in the 1850s. Photograph: Blair.*

Some names used through the years to mark white ironstone china are included in the following list:

| | |
|---|---|
| flint ware | stone granite |
| felspar china | ironstone pearl china |
| felspar opaque china | Berlin ironstone |
| stone china | Pearl china |
| granite ware | royal granite |
| opaque china | stone ware |
| ironstone china | royal patent ironstone |
| warranted stone china | royal stone china |
| imperial ironstone china | improved stone china |
| improved ironstone china | imperial white granite |
| pearl white granite | opaque porcelain |
| pearl white ironstone | royal patent ironstone |
| pearl stone ware | real stone china |

In succeeding chapters you will become acquainted with the patterns and shapes of white ironstone that were so eagerly purchased by your great, great grandmother.

### References to Explore

Klamkin, Marian. *American Patriotic and Political China*. New York: Crown Publishers, Inc., 1969.

Larsen, E. B. *American Historical Views on Staffordshire China*. New York: Doubleday & Doran, 1939. Reprinted by Dover Publications, 1979.

Little, W. L. *Staffordshire Blue*. New York: Crown Publishers, Inc., 1969.

Willis, N. P., author, and Bartlett, William H., illustrator. *American Scenery*. London: Virtue, 1838.

# III One Hundred Years of Ironstone

The patterns in this book are generally arranged chronologically with related patterns placed together. Fashions in dishes passed through different vogues as have designs in clothing through the years.

Potted in the early 1840s, the first marked white ironstone dishes were usually made in the same *Gothic Shape* used under the colored-transfer decorations of the thirties and forties. Several beautiful patterns such as Edwards' *Fluted Pearl* and *Rose Bud* designs were introduced. The unusual details of these two early patterns must have been expensive or difficult to reproduce, resulting in the manufacture of few sets. Collectors find them harder to locate than the offerings of the fifties. I still think about the fragile, handled, footed basket adorned with rose buds that the owner brought to an ironstone gathering. I've never seen another one.

By 1855, the *Sydenham Shape* and its relatives had won the hearts of American housewives and white ironstone really became "naturalized." Then English potters, clever men that they were, remembered how the Americans had clamored for the ceramic blue and white American scenes produced a few decades earlier. They began to design ironstone shapes whose names connotated Americanism: *Columbia, President, Union, LaFayette, Atlantic*, etc. Some cities were honored by marks reading *New York Shape, Paris Shape, St. Louis Shape*, or *Montpelier Shape*. Two states were highlighted in the impressed marks of *Virginia Shape* and *Kansas Shape*. Fortunate for us collectors that these labels were left to help us identify patterns. Often panels, ribs, and scallops were included in the lines most popular during these years.

Potters during the following years of the late fifties and all through the sixties, used motifs from forest leaves, orchard fruits, nuts, grains, and varied garden blooms — a sort of celebration of a succulent earth. The designs were realistic.

Roman or Greek influences were found in wreaths, well-known key designs, or fleur-de-lis lines in the late 1860s. Half a dozen patterns included narrow ribbing covering much of the body and were bordered by berries, chains, or buds. Because the registry dates were omitted in the markings, we are unable to pinpoint the age of these ribbed decorations.

Then came the Civil War and the sad years of austerity that usually follow an internal conflict. Money was short. The ironstone was no longer a novelty but the English wares were still inexpensive, so many, many more were imported. Gradually, those who could afford better, more beautiful dishes began to refer derogatively to the plain ware as "thresher's china." It was true that the people from rural areas continued to serve their food on this hardy earthenware for more decades.

As soon as the fate of the union was settled, stirrings of a strong national feeling were felt all over the American continent. Despite high tariffs, England still wooed the United States china market. A period of plain white ironstone designs was introduced. The graceful round pear-shaped bodies were generally undecorated;

rectangular shapes became popular. These changes were adopted during the 1870s and 1880s at the same time as the American pottery businesses were becoming more stable.

At the close of the century, a few more detailed designs on lighter weight white ironstone were introduced by the Staffordshire potters. Much hotel ware was made to satisfy commercial needs, but in general, the age of white ironstone popularity had passed.

3. *Fifty years of white ironstone shapes. Potted in the early 1840s, the first shapes were Gothic as shown in the upper left-hand corner. The bottom examples reveal the influences of ribs, scallops, fruits, grains, foliage, and flowers. The dishes in the upper right-hand corner were potted in the clean, simple lines of the 1880s. Photograph: Blair, Fort Plain Museum, Fort Plain, New York.*

# IV  On the Underside

How can you estimate the age of an ironstone dish? Was it English or American made? Is it an original or a reproduction? With the aid of your eyes, a magnifying glass, a little study, and much handling of old dishes, you can become quite knowledgeable.

Beware of overconfidence, however. The English potters interchanged finials on different patterns or sometimes just made a new handle because it was more expedient. Some examples of this are the three variations of the *Atlantic Shape,* small changes in the *Sydenham Shape* pitchers, the absence of the rope trim on some *Ceres Shape* covers, the two differently shaped soap dishes of the *Fig* pattern, the horizontal and the vertical toothbrush holders as found in *Ceres Shape* toilet sets, etc. I've had to retract some of my broad generalizations so I've practically banished the words "always" and "never" from my ironstone vocabulary. Saves me a lot of embarassment.

You will soon be able to recognize an old piece by its blue-white color. The later English wares and the American made pieces look creamy white when set next to the old English dishes.

*Godden's Encyclopaedia of British Pottery and Porcelain Marks* lists some general rules for reading the marks on the bottoms of dishes potted during the nineteenth century.[1] Those related to ironstone are discussed in the following paragraphs.

"Any printed mark incorporating the name of the pattern may be regarded as subsequent to 1810."

"Use of the word 'Royal' . . . suggests a date after the middle of the nineteenth century."

"Any printed mark incorporating the Royal Arms (or versions of the Arms) are 19th century or later."

"The quartered Arms without the central inescutcheon are subsequent to 1837."

"Many 19th century marks are based on stock designs-variations of Royal Arms, a garter-shaped mark (crowned or uncrowned) or the Staffordshire knot."

"The garter-shaped mark was used from 1840 onward. The Staffordshire knot may occur from about 1845 . . . much used in 1870s and 1880s . . . ." However it was not used extensively on white ironstone.

Examples of these stock designs are reproduced here.

STAFFORDSHIRE KNOT

ROYAL ARMS

GARTER

---

1. Geoffrey A. Godden, *Encyclopaedia of British Pottery and Porcelain Works* (New York: Bonanza Books, 1964), pp. 11-12.

Printed marks became popular after 1800 and were applied either before or after glazing.

Impressed marks were made by applying a metal die to the dish before the first firing. This is generally referred to as "impressed under glaze." This type of mark usually tells the collector he is holding one of the older pieces of china. However, many of the older pieces had only the black printed mark while some had both impressed and printed marks. You may have to use your magnifying glass to search for impressed letters around the rim of the base of a gravy boat, vegetable dish or open compote.

Applied marks were more rare. They were really impressed marks placed on a raised pad. The potter formed them separately from the rest of the dish he was forming and, before firing, attached the potter's identification in position on the base with the aid of a little slip for adhesive. Examples I have seen in white ironstone were potted by S. Bridgwood & Son, Richard Alcock, Burslem, and several patterns such as *Ceres, Morning Glory,* and *Laurel Wreath* by Elsmore & Forster. I'm sure you will find other examples.

By American law, the word *England* had to be affixed to imported goods after 1891. Some potters, however, had proudly marked their wares with *England* before the law was passed, so the collector will have to become acquainted with the few potters who did this. An example is the firm of J. & G. Meakin who began labeling dishes with Burslem, England as early as 1869.

*Made in England* is a twentieth century dating. *Limited, LD., Ltd,* etc. reveal a date after the 1860s but were not generally used in ceramic marks before the 1880s. *Trade Mark* had to be subsequent to the Trade Mark Act of 1862. Usually it referred to a date after 1875.[2]

Much ceramic ware produced between 1842 and 1883 bore a diamond-shaped registry mark either printed or impressed on the underside of a dish. Employed to prevent design piracy, this "bundle" contained the original design filed at the Patent Office. The date recorded the time of the introduction of the design and was not necessarily that of the date the item was potted. The protection lasted for an initial period of three years so the mark is a guide in dating. The marks generally related only to the shape and the impressed design. As a result, don't be surprised to find a *Copper Tea Leaf* or other colored decoration over a design that had already been potted in the plain white. A chart of the letters and numbers and their interpretation is included on the following page.

---

2. Ibid., p. 11.

## INDEX TO YEAR AND MONTH LETTERS

### YEARS

*1842-67*

Year Letter at Top

| | | | | | |
|---|---|---|---|---|---|
| A | = | 1845 | N | = | 1864 |
| B | = | 1858 | O | = | 1862 |
| C | = | 1844 | P | = | 1851 |
| D | = | 1852 | Q | = | 1866 |
| E | = | 1855 | R | = | 1861 |
| F | = | 1847 | S | = | 1849 |
| G | = | 1863 | T | = | 1867 |
| H | = | 1843 | U | = | 1848 |
| I | = | 1846 | V | = | 1850 |
| J | = | 1854 | W | = | 1865 |
| K | = | 1857 | X | = | 1842 |
| L | = | 1856 | Y | = | 1853 |
| M | = | 1859 | Z | = | 1860 |

*1868-83*

Year Letter at Right

| | | | | | |
|---|---|---|---|---|---|
| A | = | 1871 | L | = | 1882 |
| C | = | 1870 | P | = | 1877 |
| D | = | 1878 | S | = | 1875 |
| E | = | 1881 | U | = | 1874 |
| F | = | 1873 | V | = | 1876 |
| H | = | 1869 | W | = | Mar. 1-6 1878 |
| I | = | 1872 | | | |
| J | = | 1880 | X | = | 1868 |
| K | = | 1883 | Y | = | 1879 |

### MONTHS
### (BOTH PERIODS)

- A = December
- B = October
- C or O = January
- D = September
- E = May
- G = February
- H = April
- I = July
- K = November (and December 1860)
- M = June
- R = August (and September 1st-19th 1857)
- W = March

1842-67

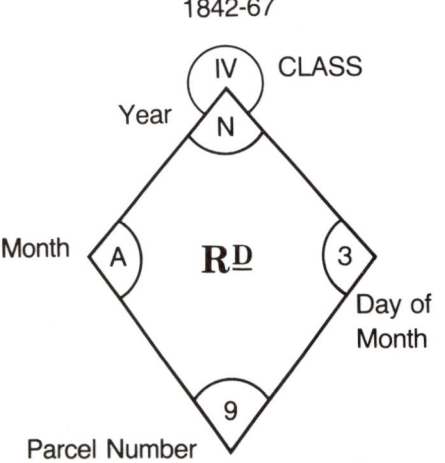

1868-83

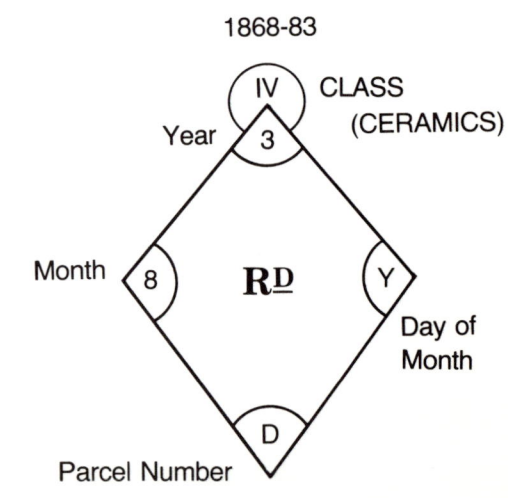

From 1884 on, designs were registered by numbers as listed below:

| | |
|---|---|
| Rd. No. 1 – Jan. 1884 | 185713 – Jan. 1892 |
| 19754 – Jan. 1885 | 205240 – Jan. 1893 |
| 40480 – Jan. 1886 | 224720 – Jan. 1894 |
| 64520 – Jan. 1887 | 246975 – Jan. 1895 |
| 90483 – Jan. 1888 | 268392 – Jan. 1896 |
| 116648 – Jan. 1889 | 291241 – Jan. 1897 |
| 141273 – Jan. 1890 | 311658 – Jan. 1898 |
| 163767 – Jan. 1891 | 331707 – Jan. 1899 |

If the number is above 360,000 the date is subsequent to 1900.

A few of the early white ironstone patterns were marked with a patent number (*Rose Bud, Line Trim,* and *Gothic*) and were also marked with the diamond-shaped registry suggesting an earlier system of numbering patents.

The word *warranted* nearly always designated American work, but here again the rule does not always prove true. For instance, the English potter, John Edwards, often marked his late nineteenth century dishes with the words WARRANTED IRONSTONE CHINA and Anthony Shaw marked his later pieces STONE CHINA WARRANTED. Yet, I repeat, the addition of *warranted* occurred most often in American ironstone marks. If you are in doubt, the best procedure is to check to see if the potter's name is included in the fairly complete list of English potters of white ironstone found in this book. If not, you probably are holding an American-made dish.

Occasionally a dish is found that gives the name of an English potter and underneath is marked "made for" with the name of an American retailer beneath. One example given in this book is the epergne pictured in Photograph 13.

Now, let's straighten out a problem that a lot of ironstone collectors have been having with each other. Each one seems to have a pattern that he *just knows* was called *Pearl*. Me too. When I really investigated, I found the word *Pearl* again and again included in the marks of nineteenth century English potters. I bring up again the fact that the famous Josiah Wedgwood made his "pearlware" in 1779 as discussed in an earlier chapter. Later potters may have been attempting to "borrow" a little of his success.

I've seen *Pearl* marked on the underside of several patterns by J. Wedgwood, in the marks of the several potters of the *Wheat and Clover* pattern, on *Scotia Shape* by F. Jones & Co., on dishes shaped by G. Phillips, W. Baker & Co., T. Walker, J. & G. Meakin, etc. Godden's *Encyclopaedia* confirmed my research with the words, "PEARL WARE or PEARL STONE WARE: Name for special earthenware body, used by many nineteenth century firms. Impressed or incorporated in printed marks."[3]

---

3. Ibid, p. 487.

Some marks simply say *Pearl* while others seem to refer more directly to the bodies with descriptions such as *Pearl China, Pearl Stone, Pearl Ironstone China, Pearl White Ironstone,* etc. Below are a few examples copied from white ironstone dishes:

T. J. & J. Mayer and the subsequent firms (Mayer Bros. & Elliot, Mayer & Elliot, and Liddle, Elliot & Son) sometimes included in their marks the words *Berlin Ironstone,* which was a name for the ironstone body used. This word so clearly marked has caused some people to think this the name of a pattern. It was printed on many different patterns.

A few kind manufacturers impressed the potting date into the body of the clay itself. Davenport marked the last two digits of the year on either side of his famous anchor. Such firms as Liddle Elliot & Son impressed two numbers, one above the other, denoting the month and year of the potting. Example: $^{11}/_{63}$ can be interpreted as November 1863. A few of the later potters simply impressed the last two digits of the year in a separate spot from the more familiar mark.

Now, we must discuss some of the confusions resulting from the name, Wedgwood, used in marks on white ironstone. The well known "prince of potters," Josiah Wedgwood, did contribute much to the development of white ironstone and his aid has been discussed elsewhere in this account. His descendants produced a "Stone China" from circa 1827 to 1861, with limited production, and marked it "Wedgwood's China" (a rare marking). However, the Josiah Wedgwood firm manufactured and usually labeled their excellent and beautiful wares simply "Wedgwood."

The inexpensive white ironstone sent to the United States in the nineteenth century was not made by this illustrious family.

Podmore, Walker, & Wedgwood of Tunstall marked their wares:

P. W. & W.   WEDGWOOD OR WEDGWOOD & CO.

Godden remarks that it was found advantageous to use the name Wedgwood alone. From about 1860, the firm was retitled, "Wedgwood & Co.," and continued on up to modern decades as "Wedgwood & Co. Ltd." until 1965 when the name was changed to "Enoch Wedgwood, Ltd." Some of the marks collectors can attribute to this company are these:

after 1862

Several very familiar patterns such as *Fig, Corn and Oats,* and *Sharon Arch* are marked J. Wedgwood. These pieces have been assigned to John Wedge Wood since the Josiah Wedgwood potteries did not use marks with the initial "J". Sometimes the marks of John Wedge Wood have a slight gap or dot between "Wedg" and "Wood." These marks have been traced to John Wedge Wood:

impressed          stamp 1841-1860          impressed

In both of these instances, the purchaser was doubtless intended to observe the familiar title and credit the products to the famous firm. This problem plagued the Wedgwood potters for generations. Other misleading marks stamped on other types of pottery through the years have been "Wedgewood," "Vedgewood," and "Wedgwood Ware" — all wares much inferior to the Wedgwood standards. If the renowned Wedgwoods ever acknowledged the inexpensive white ironstone that influenced American life, I have never been able to find an example. White ironstone potters have contributed to the Wedgwood puzzles.

Nevertheless, I have heard antique dealers proudly acclaiming, "It was made by Wedgwood," and I have been as guilty as they in adding magic and value because of a name. I hope the poor Josiahs (there were five of them) have not been too bothered by the misuse of that great Wedgwood label.

This chapter has a lot of compiled information. Can't remember it all? I can't either. I'm going to lug this book along. On the next four pages is a nearly complete list of the Staffordshire potters who produced white ironstone.

| Staffordshire Potter | Location | Date of Operation |
|---|---|---|
| Adams, Wm. & Sons | Tunstall, Stoke | 1796 – —— |
| Alcock, Henry & Co. | Cobridge | 1861 – 1910 |
| Alcock, John | Cobridge | 1853 – 1861 |
|     subsequently Henry Alcock & Co. | | |
| Alcock, Richard | Burslem | 1878 – 1883 |
|     subsequently O.J. Wilkinson | | |
| Alcock, Samuel & Co. | Cobridge | 1828 – 1853 |
| Baker, W.&Co. | Fenton | 1839 – 1932 |
| Barrow & Co. | ? | c.1850 |
| Beswick, R. | Longton | ? |
| Bishop & Stonier | Hanley | 1891 – 1939 |
| Boote, T.&R. | Burslem | 1842 – 1906 |
| Bowers, George Frederick | Tunstall | 1842 – 1868 |
| Bridgwood, S. & Sons | Longton | 1805 – —— |
| Bridgwood & Clarke | Burlsem, Tunstall | 1857 – 1864 |
|     subsequently Edw. Clarke & Co. | | |
| Brougham & Mayer | Tunstall | 1853 – 1855 |
| Brownfield, Wm.& Sons | Cobridge | 1850 – 1891 |
| Burgess, Henry | Burslem | 1864 – 1892 |
| Burgess & Goddard | Longton | c.1870 |
| Burgess & Meigh | Burslem | 1867 – 1889 |
| Challinor, C. & Co. | Fenton | 1892 – 1896 |
| Challinor, Edward | Tunstall | 1842 – 1867 |
| Challinor, E. & Co. | Fenton | 1853 – 1862 |
|     subsequently E. & C. Challinor | | |
| Challinor, E. & C. | Fenton | 1862 – 1891 |
| Clarke, Edward & Co. | Tunstall | 1865 – 1877 |
| | Longport | 1878 – 1880 |
| | Burslem | 1880 – 1887 |
| Clementson Bros. | Hanley | 1865 – 1916 |
| Clementson, Joseph | Hanley | 1839 – 1864 |
| Close & Co. | Stoke | 1855 – 1864 |
| Cockson & Chetwynd (& Co.) | Cobridge | 1867 – 1875 |
|     subsequently Cockson & Seddon | | |
| Cockson & Seddon | Cobridge | 1875 – 1877 |
| Collinson, C. & Co. | Burslem | 1851 – 1873 |
| Corn, Edward | ? | ? early |
| Corn, W. & E. | Burlsem | 1864 – 1891 |
| | Longport | 1864 – 1904 |
| Cork & Edge | Burslem | 1846 – 1860 |
| Cork, Edge, & Malkin | Burslem | 1860 – 1871 |

| | | |
|---|---|---|
| Davenport | Longport | 1793 – 1887 |
| Edge, Malkin & Co. | Burslem | 1871 – 1903 |
| Edwards, James | Burslem | 1842 – 1851 |
| Edwards, James & Son | Burslem | 1851 – 1882 |
| Edwards, John | Longton | 1847 – 1853 |
| Edwards, John | Fenton | 1853 – 1879 |
| Edwards, John  & Co. added to style | | 1873 – 1879 |
| Elsmore & Forster | Tunstall | 1853 – 1871 |
| (sometimes Forster was spelled "Foster") | | |
| Ford & Challinor | Tunstall | 1865 – 1880 |
| Forester & Hulme | Fenton | 1887 – 1893 |
| Furnival, Jacob & Co. | Cobridge | 1845 – 1870 |
| Furnival, Thomas & Co. | Hanley | 1844 – 1846 |
| Furnival, Thomas & Sons | Cobridge | 1871 – 1890 |
| Gator, Thomas & Co. | Burslem | ? |
| Gelson Bros. | Hanley | 1867 – 1876 |
| Goddard & Burgess | ? | ? |
| Goodfellow, Thomas | Tunstall | 1828 – 1859 |
| Grindley, W.H. & Co. | Tunstall | 1880 – —— |
| Hancock, Sampson & Sons | Tunstall | 1858 – 1870 |
| | Stoke | 1858 – 1937 |
| Harvey, H. & G. late | ? | ? |
| Harvey, C. & W.K. | Longton | 1835 – 1853 |
| Heath, Joseph | Tunstall | 1845 – 1853 |
| Hicks, Meigh, & Johnson | Shelton | 1822 – 1835 |
| Holland & Green | Longton | 1853 – 1882 |
| Hope & Carter | Burslem | 1862 – 1880 |
| Hughes, Thomas | Burslem | 1860 – 1894 |
| Johnson Bros. | Hanley | 1883 – —— |
| (Frederick, Lewis, & Robert) | | |
| Jones, Frederick & Sons | Longton | 1865 – 1886 |
| Jones, George | Burslem | c. 1854 |
| Jones, George & Sons | Stoke | 1861 – 1951 |
| Liddle, Elliot & Son | Longport | 1861 – —— |
| Livesley & Davis | Hanley | ? |
| Livesley, Powell & Co. | Hanley | 1851 – 1866 |
| Maddock, John | Burslem | 1842 – 1855 |
| Maddock, John & Sons | Burslem | 1855 – —— |
| Maddock & Gater | ? | ? |

| | | |
|---|---|---|
| Mayer, T.J. & J. | Burslem | 1843 – 1855 |
| subsequently Mayer Bros. & Elliot | | |
| Mayer Bros. & Elliot | Burslem | 1856 – 1858 |
| subsequently Mayer & Elliot | | |
| Mayer & Elliot | Longport | 1858 – 1861 |
| subsequently Liddle, Elliot & Son | | |
| Meakin, Alfred | Tunstall | 1875 – —— |
| Meakin Bros. | ? | ? |
| possibly same as Meakin & Co. | | |
| Meakin, Charles | Hanley | 1883 – 1889 |
| Meakin & Co. | Cobridge | 1865 – 1882 |
| Meakin, Henry | Cobridge | 1873 – 1876 |
| Meakin, J. & G. | Hanley | 1851 – —— |
| Meakin, Lewis | ? | ? |
| Meigh, Charles | Hanley | 1835 – 1849 |
| Meigh, Charles & Son | Hanley | 1851 – 1861 |
| Meigh, Charles, Son & Pankhurst | Hanley | 1850 – 1851 |
| Meir, John & Son | Tunstall | 1837 – 1897 |
| Mellor, Taylor & Co. | Burslem | 1880 – 1904 |
| Minton | Stoke | 1793 – —— |
| Morley, Francis & Co. | Hanley | 1845 – 1858 |
| Pankhurst, J.W. | Hanley | 1850 – 1851 |
| Pankhurst, J.W. & Co. | Hanley | 1852 – 1882 |
| Phillips, George | Longport | 1834 – 1848 |
| Pinder, Bourne & Co. | Burslem | 1862 – 1882 |
| Pinder, Bourne & Hope | Burlsem | 1851 – 1862 |
| Podmore, Walker & Co. | Tunstall | 1834 – 1859 |
| subsequently Wedgwood & Co. | | |
| Powell & Bishop | Hanley | 1876 – 1878 |
| Powell, Bishop & Stonier | Hanley | 1878 – 1891 |
| Proctor, John | Longton | 1843 – 1846 |
| Ridgway, Bates & Co. | Hanley | 1856 – 1858 |
| Ridgway, John & Co. | Hanley | 1830 – 1855 |
| Ridgway, Wm. & Co. | Shelton, Hanley | 1830 – 1854 |
| Ridgway, Wm. & Son & Co. | Hanley | 1838 – 1848 |
| Shaw, Anthony (& Co.) | Tunstall | 1851 – 1856 |
| (& Son) | Burslem | 1860 – c.1900 |
| Taylor, W. | Hanley | ? |
| Turner, Goddard & Co. | Tunstall | 1867 – 1874 |
| Turner, G. W. & Sons | Tunstall | 1873 – 1895 |
| Turner & Tomkinson | Tunstall | 1860 – 1872 |

| | | |
|---|---|---|
| Venables, John | Burslem | c.1853 – 1855 |
| Walley, Edward | Cobridge | 1845 – 1856 |
| Walker, Thomas | ? | ? |
| Wedgwood & Co. | Tunstall | 1860 – —— |
|     formerly Podmore, Walker & Co. (& Wedgwood) | | |
| Wedgwood, J. (see John Wedge Wood) | | |
| Wilkinson, Arthur J. | Burlsem | 1885 – —— |
| Wilkinson & Hulme | Burslem | 1883 – 1885 |
|     subsequently Arthur J. Wilkinson | | |
| Wood & Hulme | Burslem | 1882 – 1905 |
| Wood, John Wedge | Burslem, Tunstall | 1841 – 1860 |
|     printed mark "J. Wedgwood" | | |
| Wood & Son(s) | Burslem | 1865 – —— |
| Wood, Son & Co. | Cobridge | 1869 – 1879 |
| Wood, Rathbone & Co. | Cobridge | ? |
| Wooliscroft, George | Tunstall | 1851 – 1853 |
|     this name occurs with one and two "l"s. | Tunstall | 1860 – 1864 |

| **Scottish Potters** | **Location** | **Date of Operation** |
|---|---|---|
| Bell, J. & M.R. & Co. | Glasgow | 1842 – 1928 |
| Cochran, Robert & Co. | Glasgow | 1846 – 1918 |

| **Derbyshire Potters** | **Location** | **Date of Operation** |
|---|---|---|
| Pearson, E. & Co. | Chesterfield | 1805 – —— |
| Bourne, Joseph | Denby | 1833 – 1860 |

# V  The Process of Potting

*Do thou, thrice happy England, flill prepare Thy clay, and build thy fame on* Earthenware.

From "Isabella" by Sir Charles Hanbury Williams

The cheap, durable earthenware dishes of the nineteenth century were manufactured chiefly by the English potters of the Staffordshire area and used both for home consumption and for exportation to various part of the world.

The most common body, *China Stone,* consisted of Dorset or Poole clay, Cornish or Devonian kaolin, and flint. The above clay was a weathered pegmatite used to give hardness and a vitreous nature to the fired substance. A better body, *China Clay,* was made of the same ingredients except that the Dorset or Poole clay used had been produced by the decomposition of granite used in *China Stone.* The proportions used of clay, kaolin, and flint were discovered by Cookworthy in Cornwall.

Each substance had its own preparation. The *Dorset* or *Poole clay,* the chief ingredient, was mixed with water, passed through sieves of different sizes, cleared of lumps and finally rendered to a fine consistency. The *kaolin* needed no cleaning process. The *flints* were used as they came, passed through grinding mills, then finely reduced to minute particles in water and drained. This combination of materials made up the *China Stone* or *China Clay.*

This *China Stone* was then calcined or burnt in kilns, crushed, and reduced to fine powder in mills. Then it was ready to be used.

The proportions were different for different wares. Water was mixed with the prepared elements and the resulting mixture was taken to the *slip-kiln,* a long brick trough heated by flues from a furnace. There the mixture was kept simmering to evaporate the water until a doughlike substance issued. Cobalt oxide was then added to the mixed clay if the potter desired a whiter product. This potter's clay was stored in a cold dark cellar until needed.

*Molds* had been largely employed in the making of white salt-glazed products and their use continued on into the age of ironstone. These molds were usually made of plaster of paris. The potter's clay was first rolled into flattened pieces which could be easily pressed or cast into a mold by hand. (This separate treatment may explain why so many covers and lids fit rather poorly or only in certain positions.) Small pieces such as decorations or handles were often forced into *thumb molds* with the pressure of the thumb naturally. Intricate pieces were made in parts from separate molds and then the parts were joined together afterward by a little slip. Then they were all fired as one unit. The thick *slip* was merely the potter's clay mixed with a little water and applied much as a housewife uses water to attach an extra piece of pie crust.

The Edwards dish below is a probable example of ware that was molded in six pieces: the body of the bowl, the cover, the two handles, the gourd finial, and the hollow base ring.

After shaping, the forms were taken to be carefully dried in rooms prepared for the purpose. Here much of the water content was lost which facilitated the future handling.

When dry enough, the pieces were placed in large flat-bottomed pans, either oval or round, with vertical sides. These were called *seggars* and were constructed of refractory materials such as fire clays, broken earthenware, broken seggars, or damaged clays. The forms were packed as closely as possible without injury to one another. The seggars were arranged one above the other in a kiln.

The *kiln* or oven was fired until the proper heat was reached. The fire was continued for three days. A kiln fired on Monday was ready "to be drawn" (the seggars removed) on Friday morning. The pottery at this stage was known as biscuit, fired but not glazed.

The lead *glazes* were discontinued on tablewares because of the toxic danger. The salt glazes were easy to apply (just salt cast into the kiln filled with forms) but the resultant pottery had a pitted finish undesirable in table services. An excellent feldspar glaze was perfected but included borax which cost so much that it was used only on costly services until after the early 1830s. The principal ingredient was feldspar ground to a fine powder. The published recipe, which was not patented and remained free to all, was "27 felspar, 18 borax, 4 Lynn sand, 3 nitre, 3 soda, 3 Cornwall china clay." This was melted to a frit and ground to a fine powder with 3 parts of calcined borax added before grinding. As far as I can ascertain, the tough glaze on white ironstone was made from similar materials.

Varying according to the potter, the materials of the *glaze* were mixed with water to the consistency of cream. The bisuit earthenware was skillfully dipped into this creamy solution. The water sank into the porous body and a thin coating of the pulverized materials of the glaze remained. Then the dish was placed in a *gloss kiln* for one day. The gloss kiln was subjected to less heat than the biscuit kiln; there was just sufficient heat to reduce the coating to a layer of glass. This glaze was necessary to hinder the access of liquids to the unprotected earthenware beneath.

These are the processes by which those ambitious Staffordshire potters produced set after set of gleaming blue-white dishes and chamber sets for the homes of America.

# VI  What's in a Set?

A great amount of speculation goes on concerning the original uses of unusual white ironstone dishes. I have found that the early potters were not as unchangeable in their potting rules as are ardent collectors in their generalizations. I have learned to reiterate, "I just don't know. Do you suppose it could have been this way or that?" Therefore, the information in the following paragraphs is not complete, just a setting down of such facts as have been uncovered.

A 1827 sale list included these pieces as parts of a set of dishes:

        2 soup tureens with covers and stands
        6 sauce tureens with covers and stands
        4 vegetable dishes with covers
        19 dishes in sizes (platters or relish dishes?)
        2 fish plates
        60 table plates
        18 soup plates
        48 pie plates

Without seeing an actual complete set, we can only speculate. Certainly the sixty table plates must not have been all the same size. What about cups? One of our dear old neighbors, more than ninety years young, told me that he remembered that his mother had had two sets of "wheat ironstone" that she used to feed hop pickers at harvest time. Do you suppose it could have been one enormous set similar to the one described above?

Open elongated octagonal, rectangular, or oval servers in various sizes were called *bakers*. One occasionally comes across the term, *twiffler* or *twyffler*. I have heard it defined as a "middle-sized plate" or "a pudding plate" or the pewter piece we usually call a porringer. In 1842, a "twiffle-maker" was described as a "maker of small plates." All of which proves that I'm not sure of what a twiffler was, but I think there were white ironstone twifflers made.

Handleless cups were probably derived from the Oriental tea bowls still used today in the Far East. They were cheaper to pot and more apt to survive ocean voyages than their handled cousins. Most early ironstone sets included handleless cups in two sizes: a seven and a-half ounce teacup with its six-inch saucer and a ten-ounce coffee cup with its six-and-a-half inch saucer. Cup plates, a little more than four inches in diameter, were usual parts of a set. Those little shallow dishes, a little deeper and wider than cup plates — what were they used for? I've heard all sorts of authoritative answers. A honey dish. Oh, no, they were just a deeper saucer so that our forefathers could cool their tea before sipping it. What do you think?

I have seen handled cups in the *Sydenham Shape, Ceres Shape,* and *Sharon Arch,* so some orders must have been filled with this change from the usual handleless cups. By 1875, most sets had handles on the cups and also the number of pieces in a set was smaller. By this time, too, covered butter dishes, butter pats, and bone dishes were often included as parts of a table setting.

Collectors prize a complete tea set comprised of graceful teapot, its companion creamer and large sugar bowl, a deep waste bowl, and the cups and saucers. Some sets include both the teapot and the larger coffeepot as shown in Photograph 5.

Pitchers (or jugs as they were first called) came in many different sizes from the little creamer to the towering water ewer in toilet sets. Photograph 8 depicts a parade of *Sydenham* pitchers from five inches to twelve and three-quarter inches high. The *President* pattern too included many sized pitchers.

Toothbrush holders came in several different shapes, sometimes even in the same pattern. For instance, the *Ceres Shape* made both a vertical and a horizontal brush holder. Different sized soap holders were made in the same design. A small rectangular container and a large round soapdish have both been seen several times in *Fig*. Those Staffordshire men were quite able to adapt to the whims of the American housewife.

4. Nautilus shell spoon warmer, a Victorian solution to frigid morning air and quick-cooling porridge. Most warmers were silver-plated, made around the turn of the century. "Some few were made of sterling silver, some of Britannia ware, and occasional ones of porcelain, the latter so highly prized that former owners had them mended in case of breakage."[1] The nautilus shell was the most popular shape. Nautical designs including buoys, seaweed, coral, tritons, and bi-valve shells such as oyster or the scallop shape used above were employed. This early ironstone warmer, circa 1880, was acquired by Mr. and Mrs. John Black. Photograph: Black.

5. VICTOR SHAPE tea set by F. Jones, minus the sugar bowl. Photographed from the collection of Mr. and Mrs. Gary Grove, Pennsylvania.

6. MORNING GLORY fruit dish, 2½" high and 11¼" in diameter, is from the collection of James and Doris Walker, New York. Photograph: Blair.

---

1. Dorothy T. Rainwater, "Spoon Warmers," *Spinning Wheel*, October 1977, p. 35.

One more puzzle. Three or four times I have located a large low dish, about two and a-half inches high and eleven and a fourth inches in diameter. I have no idea as to its original purpose but my fellow collectors have lots of ideas: a fruit dish, a community mush bowl, a child's wash bowl, and so on. I just don't know but I sure could find a use for one if I acquire one of those "whatcha-call-it-bowls." (See Photograph 6.)

I have also seen a hot dish server in *Tuscan Shape*. It was deep, very much like a large soup plate, and had an arched cover to keep the hot cakes warm. Another collector owns an unusual plate warmer with double bottom and hole to add hot water. (See Photograph 102.)

Some day we'll combine our pictures of unusual ironstone pieces in a scrapbook to help us remember. Meanwhile we'll just keep on learning what can be found "in a set."

*7. WHEAT AND CLOVER teapot and larger coffeepot collected by Mr. and Mrs. Gary Grove, Pennsylvania.*

*8. SYDENHAM pitchers from 5" to 12¾" high. There are slight differences in some borders. Collection of Mr. and Mrs. James Walker. Photograph: Blair.*

9. *Plates with concaved decor. From left to right: FULL RIBBED by J. W. Pankhurst, FLUTED PEARL by J. Wedgwood, and TRUE SCALLOP by J. Edwards. Photograph: Blair.*

10. *Toothbrush holders came in various shapes. Notice here that the CERES holders were potted in both vertical and horizontal shapes as shown by the two dishes to the left. From the collection of Mrs. Jane Diemer of Delaware.*

# VII  Earliest White Ironstone

All-white ironstone first appeared shortly after 1840. The *Gothic* family shapes with hexagonal and octagonal lines had already been used by Staffordshire potters as bases for the cobalt and mulberry transfer wares. The new idea caught on. Certainly the all-white was cheaper to produce and was a welcome change from the busier, colored patterns. Most successful potters of the period manufactured some dinner sets in their own version of the *Gothic* shape. Human profiles, roses, lilies, etc. varied the finials or the trim under handles.

Nearly half of the early patterns listed in this book were created by the firm of James Edwards of Burslem. His variety of designs were remarkable.

The firm of T. J. & J. Mayer won a prize for their white ironstone in 1851. Many of their wares included the words "Prize Medal" in their marks on the undersides of their dishes. Among these are *Prize Puritan* and *Prize Bloom*.

A line of scallops is found in three patterns early in the 1850s: *Adam's Scallop*, *Line Trim* by Edwards, and *Scalloped Decagon* by both Davenport and J. Wedgwood. (Note how often Davenport and J. Wedgwood used the same pattern in the years that followed. Were they cooperating or was one of them adept at piracy?)

The highly original *Fluted Pearl*, registered in 1847 by J. Wedgwood, and *Fig*, made by both Davenport and J. Wedgwood after 1856, are both among the most collectible patterns. I am glad that I was able to locate enough pieces so that the photographs can introduce you to their beauties.

*11. GOTHIC chowder tureen with plateau liner and ladle, registered by T. J. & J. Mayer in 1847. It dwells in a corner of an old country restaurant, Saltzman's Hotel, Ephratah, New York. The 5½" creamer by James Edwards was also registered in 1847 with an accompanying No. 44036. Photograph: Blair.*

**Gothic,** an early pattern used by many different potters in the 1840s and 1850s. Some makers were the Mayers, Ridgway, Davenport, James Edwards, etc.

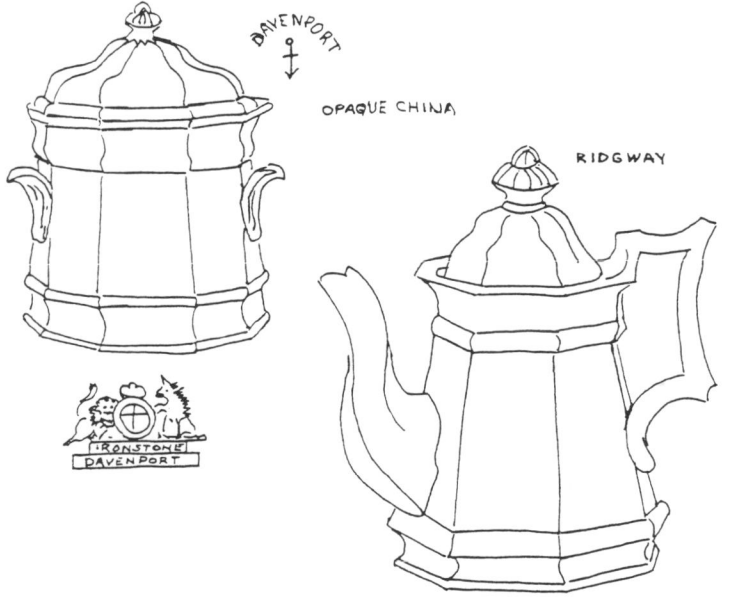

12. GOTHIC SHAPE carafe made by J.F. (?). Collection of Doris and James Walker, New York. Photograph: Blair.

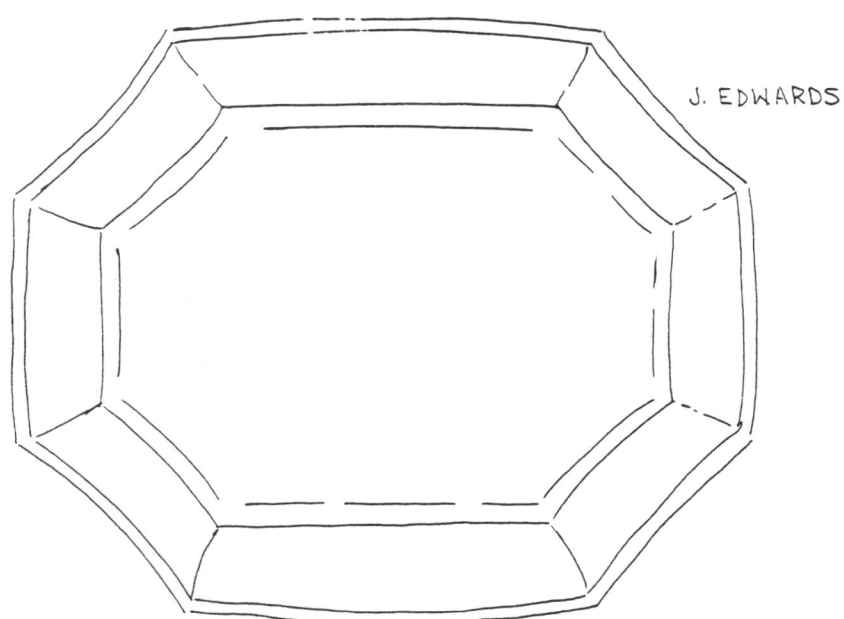

**Curved Gothic** by James Edwards, registered 1843, the earliest diamond-shaped registry mark that I have seen on white ironstone.

13. CURVED GOTHIC epergne, 14" tall. "Manufactured for E. A. & S. R. Tilley, St. Louis, Mo. by T. J. & J. Mayer, Longport," on bottom. Owned by Mr. and Mrs. John Black, New York. Photograph: Black.

**Berlin Swirl** T. J. & J. Mayer and their successors, Mayer & Elliott, and Liddle, Elliott & Son all made this popular pattern. A soup tureen manufactured by the first firm above was marked 1845 while the plate at left was impressed 1864. It was unusual for a design to be used for so many years.

**Fluted Pearl** J. Wedgwood, clearly dated 1847.

14. FLUTED PEARL pattern by J. Wedgwood marked with diamond-shaped registry and "registered 1847." Collection of James and Doris Walker. Photograph: Blair.

15. FLUTED PEARL vegetable tureen by John Wedgwood was used by Mrs. Adin Van Wie to serve her husband's beef stew. Photograph: LeBel.

**Rose Bud** James Edwards, marked in an unusual manner with No. 56632 and the additional words "Registered Dec. 16th. 1848 by James Edwards." This pattern is square-shaped with flat beveled corners; the covers are capped with big rosebuds.

16. *Square soup tureen with liner and ladle, registered in 1848 by James Edwards. The square corners appear to be cut off and a large rosebud is the finial shape. Collection of Mr. and Mrs. William Horner. Photograph: Dr. Horner.*

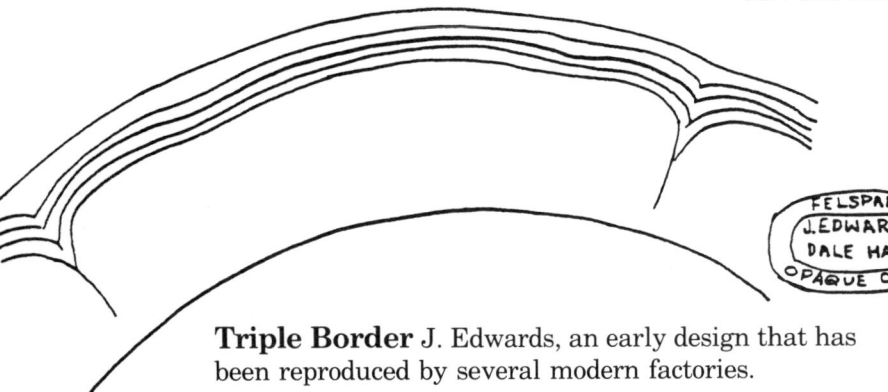

**Triple Border** J. Edwards, an early design that has been reproduced by several modern factories.

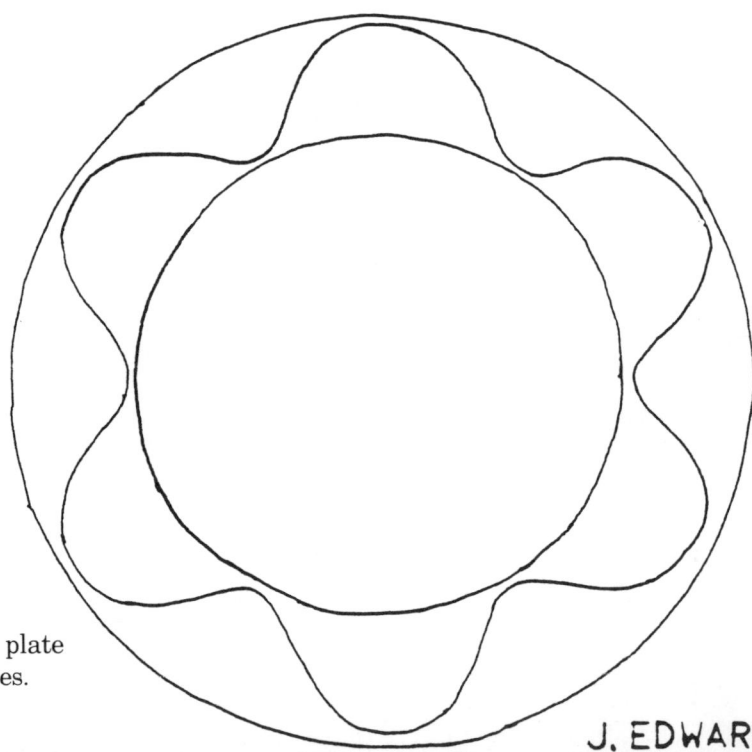

**Rolling Star** J. Edwards. This is an unusual plate with three-dimensional planes forming the curves.

*17. PRIZE PURITAN by T. J. & J. Mayer, registered 1851.*

**Cone on Fern** (name illegible) John Alcock, registered 1853.

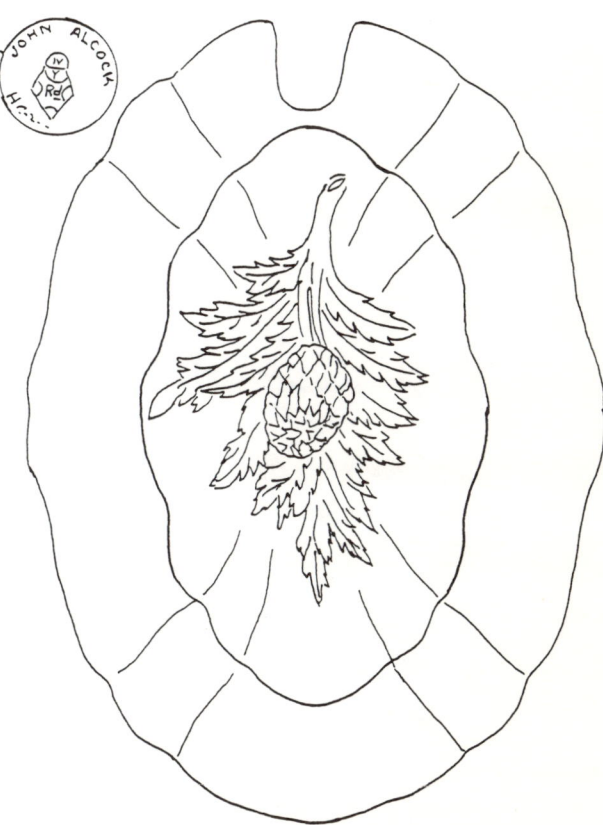

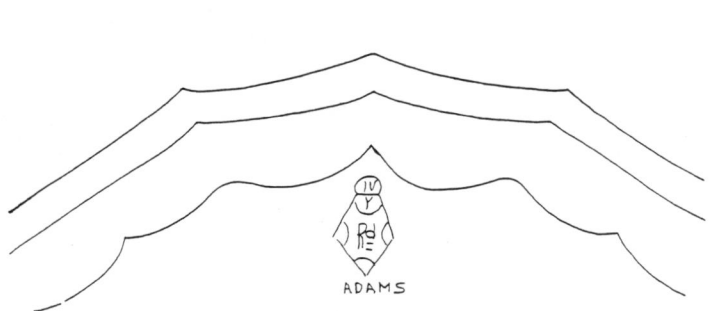

**Adam's Scallop** William Adams, registered 1853.

*18. ADAM'S SCALLOP tureen, 11" long with cone finial, registered 1853. Photograph: Blair.*

**Line Trim** J. Edwards, also G. Wooliscroft.

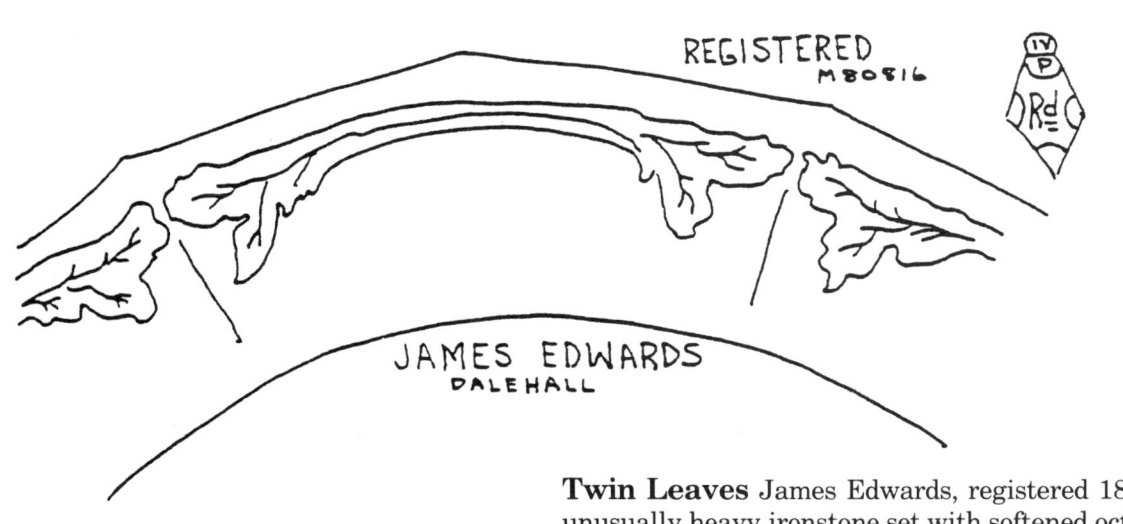

**Twin Leaves** James Edwards, registered 1851. An unusually heavy ironstone set with softened octagonal lines. The sugar bowl is hexagonal with a rosebud finial.

**Scalloped Decagon** Davenport, registered 1853, but potted in 1856 as proved by the numbers on either side of the well-known Davenport anchor. J. Wedgwood also used this design.

19. SCALLOPED DECAGON (a design potted by both J. Wedgwood and Davenport) creamer and large ewer from a toilet set owned by Mr. and Mrs. John Black. Photograph: Black.

**Unnamed Plate** by T. J. & J. Mayer.

43

**Gothic Rose** C. Meigh & Son.

20. GOTHIC CAMEO tureen registered in 1847. This same cameo motif was used on mulberry and blue transfer china. Photograph: Blair.

20A. Close-up of cameo head below handle of GOTHIC CAMEO tureen.

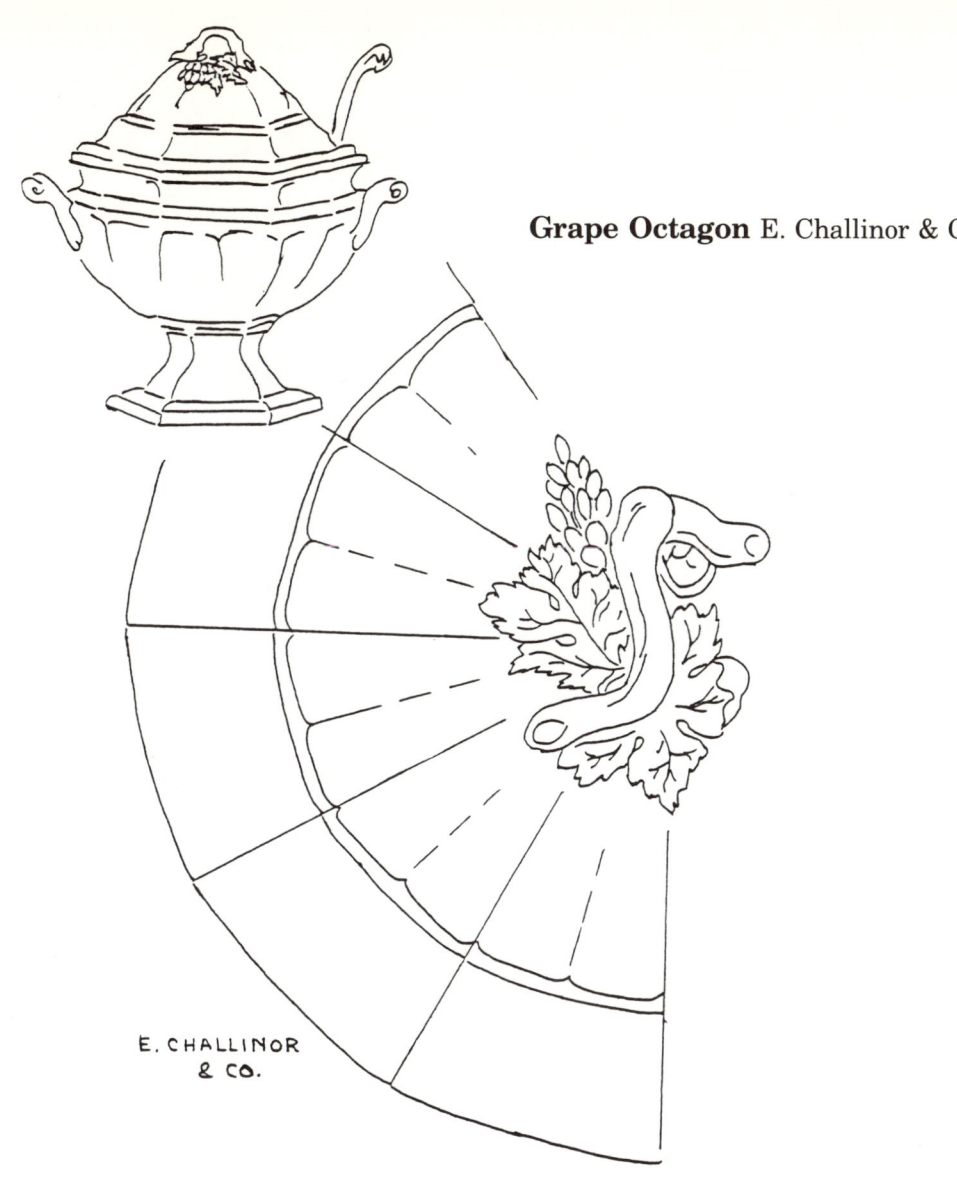

**Grape Octagon** E. Challinor & Co.

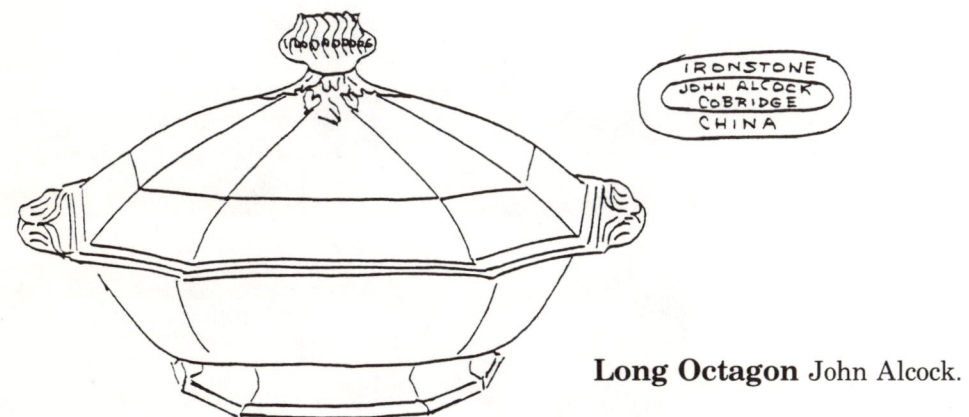

**Long Octagon** John Alcock.

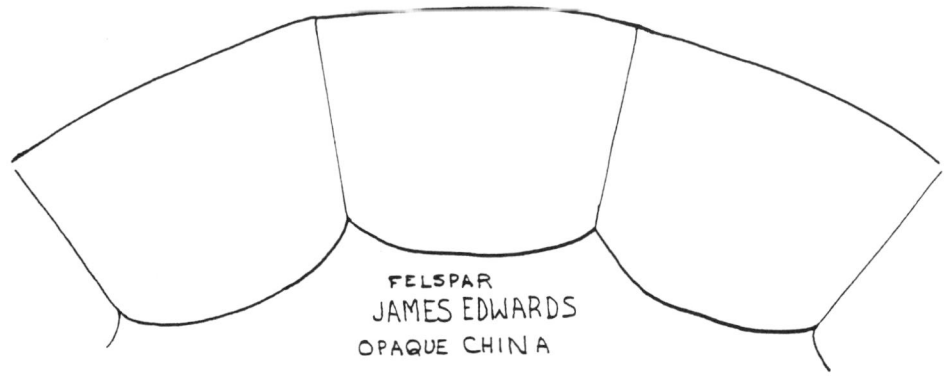

**True Scallop** James Edwards.

**Fig** J. Wedgwood, also Davenport, registered 1856.

21. FIG dishes potted by J. Wedgwood or Davenport. From a exhibit at the Fort Plain Museum, Fort Plain, New York. Photograph: Blair.

22. PRIZE BLOOM by T. J. & J. Mayer, a hexagonal shape with twelve concave panels and an extraordinary flower finial. Registered in 1853, owned by Mr. and Mrs. John Black. Photograph: Black.

22A. PRIZE BLOOM teapot from the collection of James and Doris Walker. Photograph: Walker.

23. Early sauce tureen by J. Edwards introduced the split pod as a decoration on top, a practice used by later potters and now identified as SPLIT POD. Photograph: Black.

# VIII Sydenham and Similar Shapes

The American housewife of the mid-nineteenth century was pleased to be able to order an entirely new ironstone pattern offered for sale by T. & R. Boote of Burslem. Not only did it promise to be practical enough to survive the rigors of her life in the most remote areas but also appealed to her desire for beauty. It still appeals to collectors all over the country as they hoard their finds in overflowing cupboards. Champions of this *Sydenham* have been known to keep their dining tables permanently set in these graceful dishes while they eat in the kitchen.

In 1842, Thomas and Richard Boote purchased the Waterloo Pottery and other works in Burslem and there perfected a new method of making floor tiles. They also made dinner services in ironstone and worked at producing the new Parian Ware which was becoming popular.

In 1850, the Bootes put up a new factory in which was shaped the first pattern of the heavier *Sydenham*-types. This has been simply nicknamed *Boote's 1851 Octagon Shape,* as taken from the registry date and lines. It was the forerunner of the now famous *Sydenham Shape.* The *Octagon* had a simpler border with deeper dishes and also introduced the ring-handled teapots. (See Photograph 37.) All of these serving pieces now sell for as much as the coveted Sydenham pieces.

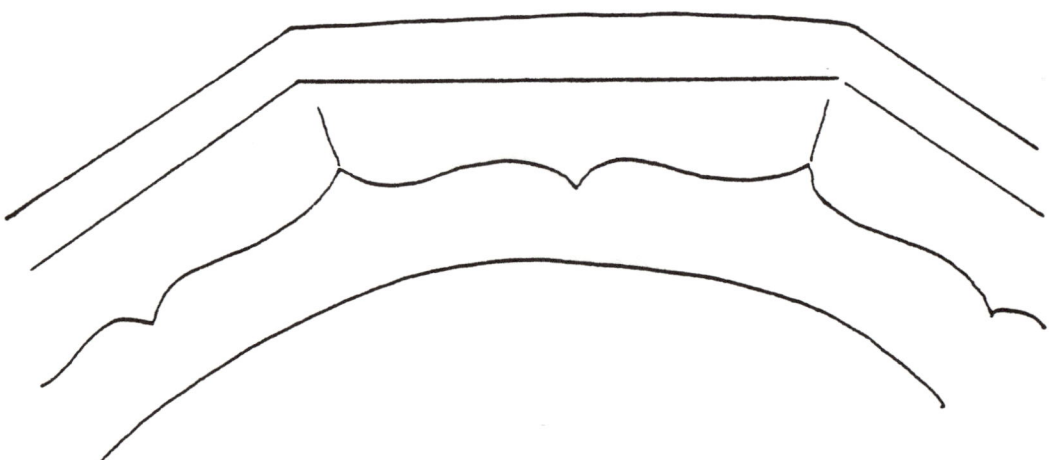

**Boote's 1851 Octagon** T. & R. Boote, registered 1851. Plates repeat motif ten times.

Echoing closely many of the *1851 Octagon* lines, the Bootes brought out their *Sydenham Shape* in 1853. They registered it again with small changes in 1854.

Just why the name *Sydenham* was chosen is unknown. It was the name of an old English family. Joseph Clementson and his partner, Reed, also made dinnerware for the American markets at a Hanley firm called The Sydenham Works. Clementson marked a flow blue pattern by this name before white ironstone became popular. In 1851, there was a great fair held in the suburb of London named Sydenham. Perhaps one of these facts had an influence on the choice of the name.

Many sizes of *Sydenham* plates were manufactured in both octagonal and round shapes, from large ten-inch plates down to tiny four-and-one-half inch cup plates. Platters and open vegetable servers, called bakers, were potted in oval or long octagonal lines. These bakers came in many sizes varying from the generous deep one shown in Photograph 24 to small seven-inch ones.

The motif on sugar bowls, pitchers, handleless cups, and the rare pedestaled syllabub cups depicted the elongated leaf folded back over the vertical panels.

24. Boote's 1851 OCTAGON SHAPE, *forerunner of the famous* SYDENHAM SHAPE. *Platter and baker are 12" long. Photograph: Blair.*

25. SYDENHAM SHAPE *sugar bowl, creamer, and 10" plate by T. & R. Boote. Probably the most collectible pattern, with beautiful octagonal lines. Collection of James and Doris Walker, New York. Photograph: Blair.*

As you can see in Photograph 28 the nickname, *Tulip Shape Sydenham* was prompted by the sweeping curved lines of the covered vegetable servers and tureens. Fortunate indeed is the collector who owns a graduated set of vegetable dishes or a giant soup tureen, complete with liner and ladle, and its exact mimic in miniature, a sauce tureen. (See Photograph 26.)

There were two gravy boats made, one definitely echoing the tulip lines, and the other marked *Sydenham* with the folded leaf decoration.

The relish or pickle dishes were leaf-shaped. A *Sydenham* collector in southern New York has a stack of a dozen in which she serves her individual salads. All are marked *Sydenham Shape*. Similar ones are sometimes impressed *Columbia Shape* or simply marked with the potter's name as is the one potted by Clementson shown on page 127.

Pause long enough to study the picture of the unusual twelve-inch oval serving dish in Photograph 27. This had a large fruit finial surrounded by much foliage, not used on the round servers. There were smaller sizes made.

This Boote pattern must have been successful with American housewives for, within a few years, many potters copied the lines in what I will now call the Sydenham-type patterns. I have found some pieces of white ironstone by J. Clementson clearly marked *Sydenham Shape*. These are few.

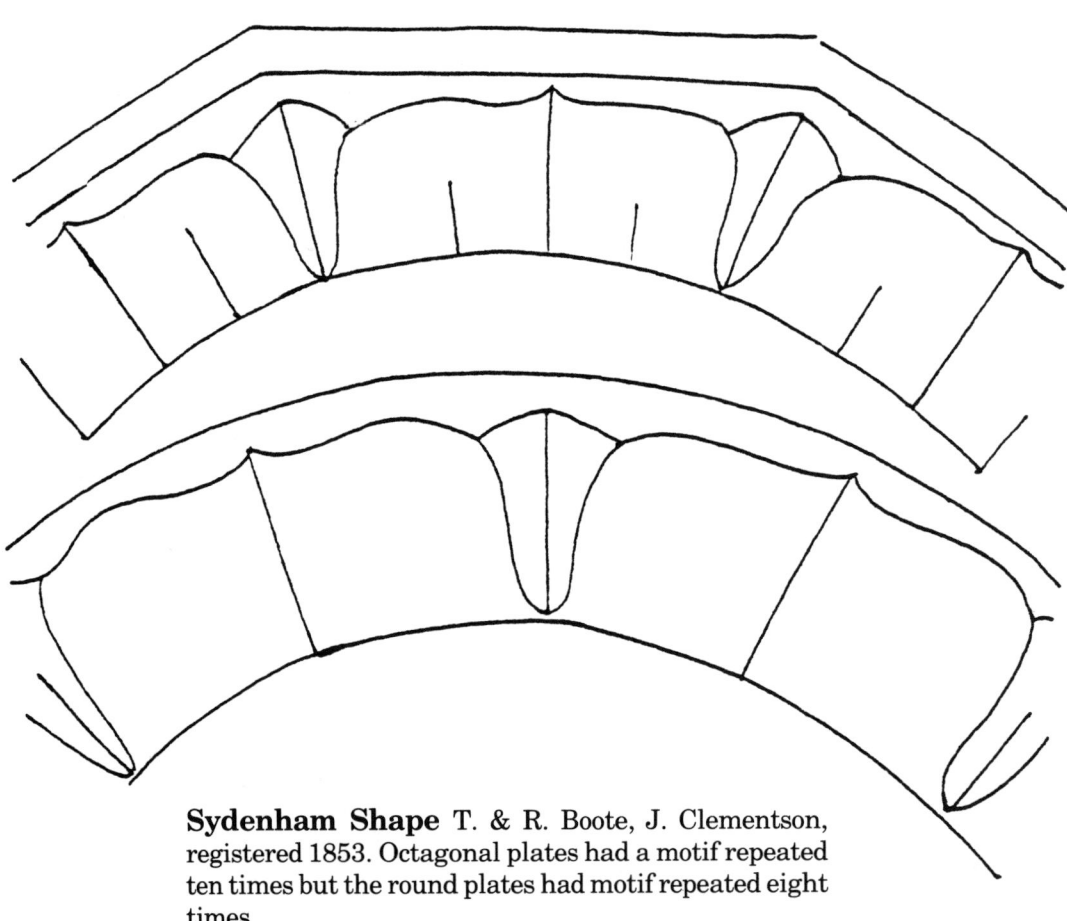

**Sydenham Shape** T. & R. Boote, J. Clementson, registered 1853. Octagonal plates had a motif repeated ten times but the round plates had motif repeated eight times.

**26. SYDENHAM SHAPE** soup tureen, complete with liner and ladle, is flanked by matching sauce tureens. All of the pieces in this remarkable grouping are from the collection of Mr. and Mrs. John Black. Photograph: Black.

**27. SYDENHAM** oval tureen, 12", discovered in the china closet of Saltsman's country restaurant in the historic Mohawk Valley. Photograph: Blair.

**28. TULIP SYDENHAM** serving dishes, characterized by sweeping upward lines. The J.F. gravy boat is not SYDENHAM but is used here to show how certain lines of this pattern influenced later designs. Photograph: Blair.

**29. SYDENHAM** toilet set offered by Boote. Here is a complete marked set, except for the absent mug and the substitute cover on the chamber (an 1851 OCTAGON). These prizes are placed beside an old spool bed in the home of James and Doris Walker who live in the foothills of the Adirondack Mountains. Photograph: Blair.

In 1855 and again in 1856, J. Edwards registered his *President Shape*. Both oval and round shapes were used in the serving dishes with varied finials and foliage for each.

The simple squatty *President* pitchers and teapot have six vertical rounded panels, each grooved in the center, and ending near the neck with the same curves impressed on the plates. Pauline Meissen-Helter described "a large oval fruit bowl with a pedestal base and big embossed oak leaves spreading to each side of the body from closed scrolled handles."[1]

I enjoy raving about a three-and-one-half quart *President* syllabub bowl and matching cups. I gave the cups a ride from Boston to Rochester to get their pictures taken with the mother bowl. Naturally, neither collector will give up their rare pieces so I'm afraid it was a one day reunion. Beautiful, beautiful, beautiful. (See Photograph 31.)

30. PRESIDENT *oval serving dish by James Edwards uses decor similar to the* SYDENHAM SHAPE. *Collection of Karl and Linda Dalenberg, Massachusetts. Photograph: Blair.*

31. PRESIDENT SHAPE *syllabub or toddy bowl, 3½ quart, with matching cups. The bowl is owned by the Blacks in New York and the Dalenbergs in Massachusetts possess the cups. Photograph: Black.*

**President Shape** J. Edwards, registered 1855 and again in 1856. Both round and oval shapes were used in serving dishes.

---

1. Pauline Meissen-Helter, "What Is Ironstone," (unpublished).

In my first little ironstone handbook, I asked the question, "Can anyone write me if the company name is legible on your *Columbia* prize?" The response was surprising. Ironstone fans hastened to educate me by telephone and letters complete with photographs and drawings. These potters of *Columbia Shape* have been verified many times over: Livesley & Powell, J. Clementson, E. & C. Challinor, G. Wooliscroft, J. Meir & Son, and Elsmore & Foster. (I thought the first few collectors were unable to copy letters correctly on this last spelling, until I ran into "Foster," instead of "Forster" clearly impressed on three different pieces. Since I can find no record of such a firm, I wonder if the stamp was in error.) The *Columbia Shape* was registered in 1855.

**Columbia Shape** Livesley & Powell, J. Clementson, E. & C. Challinor, G. Wooliscroft, J. Meir & Son, and Elsmore & Foster (not Forster), registered 1855.

32. COLUMBIA SHAPE sauce tureen with applelike fruit decoration. Owned by James and Doris Walker, New York. Photograph: Blair.

The design around the *Columbia* plates is more deeply impressed than in the *President*. Otherwise the two plate patterns are exactly the same except that the center line in the leaves of the *Columbia* is slightly split at the end, allowing us to distinguish between the two plates. Note that detail in the border of the round sauce tureen.

Each *Columbia* potter used the same border on the plates and platters. Their originality was made evident in the varied finials and foliage decorations. Notice the pod finial chosen by E. & C. Challinor to grace their soup tureen shown in Photograph 33. (Watch closely because you'll see the same finial used on other patterns.)

33. COLUMBIA SHAPE *soup tureen by E. & C. Challinor, 15" long and nearly 13" tall with a large pod finial.* SYDENHAM *cup and saucer included. Both from the collection of James and Doris Walker, New York. Photograph: Blair.*

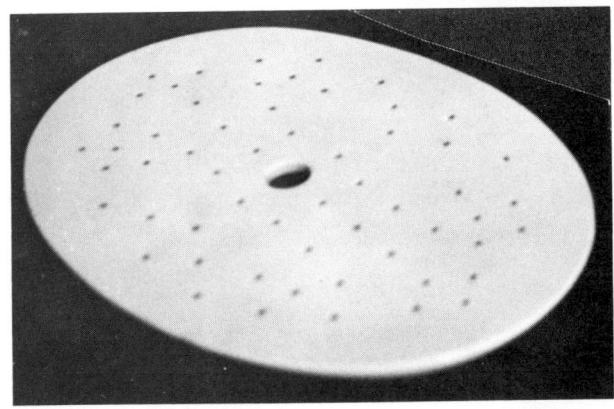

34. COLUMBIA SHAPE *well-and-tree platter with perforated liner is a rare piece and was potted by Clementson. Owners are Mr. and Mrs. William Horner. Photograph: Dr. Horner.*

Another related pattern registered in 1855 was marked with three different names. J. Clementson called his *Dallas Shape;* T. Hulme, J. Meir, G. Bowers and G. Wooliscroft labeled their round and octagonal plates *Baltic Shape;* E. Pearson, a Derbyshire potter, stamped his *Mississippi Shape.* These lines reverse the lines of *Sydenham,* having the leaf hang down rather than point up.

In the following chapter, you will sometimes recognize the tulip lines, the familiar panels, or the pointed leaf as found in the *Sydenham* patterns of the fifties.

It seems odd that this popular pattern and its imitations were not repeated in the following decades but we do not find them.

Has all this propaganda made a *Sydenham* fan out of you? Let's go search for a *Sydenham* dish to liven the display on your pine hutch.

**Dallas Shape** J. Clementson, registered 1855.

**Mississippi Shape** E. Pearson, registered 1855.

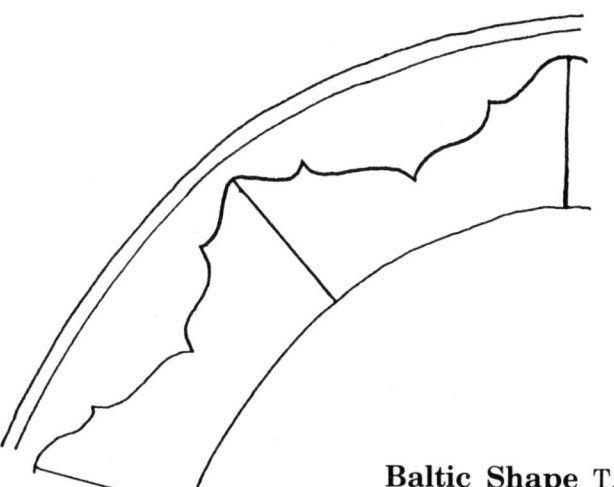

**Baltic Shape** T. Hulme, J. Meir, G. Bowers, G. Wooliscroft, registered 1855. Plates were made in both round and octagonal shapes.

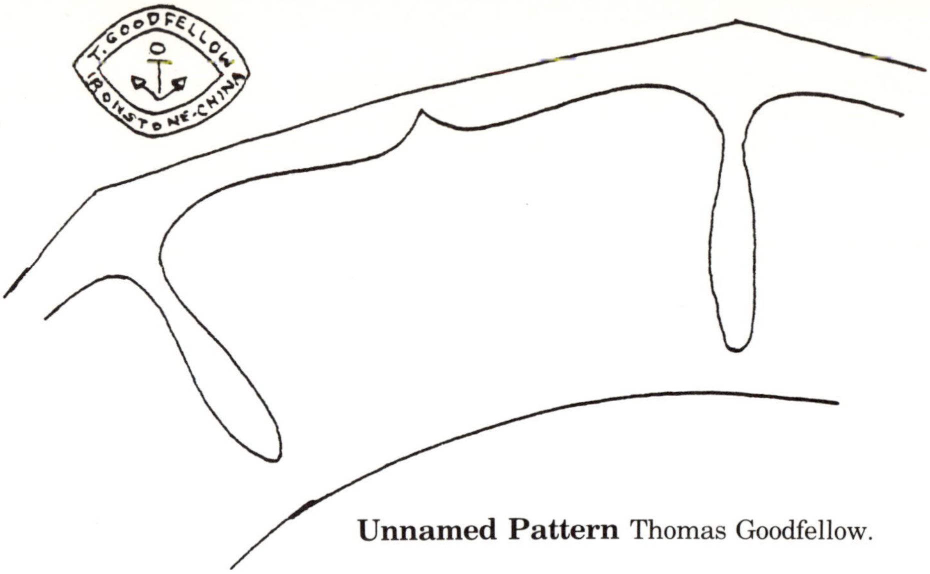

**Unnamed Pattern** Thomas Goodfellow.

**Wrapped Sydenham** W. E. Corn.

**Double Sydenham** Livesley & Powell.

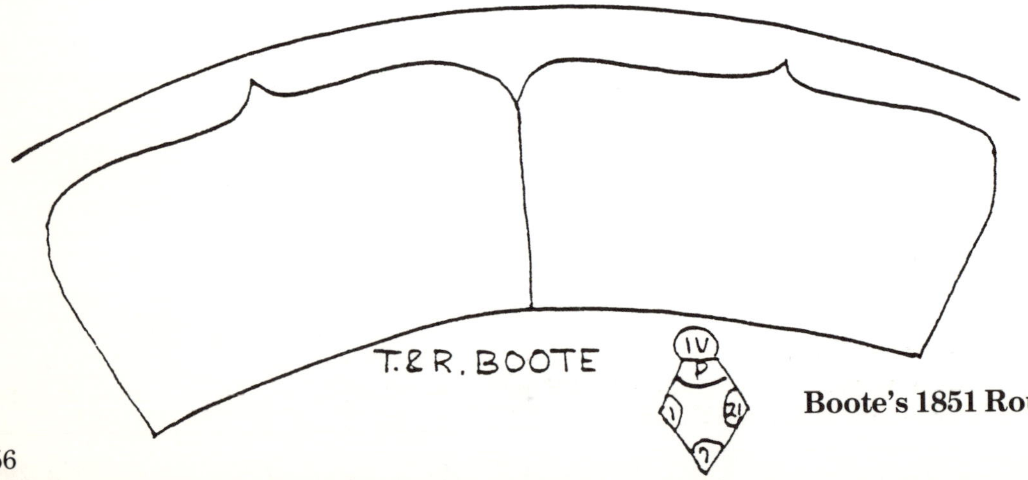

**Boote's 1851 Round** T. & R. Boote, registered 1851.

**Panelled Lily** Marked J. F. This dish echoes the shape introduced by the SYDENHAM TULIP in their vegetable servers.

*35. Syrup dispenser in SYDENHAM-type design. Sugar bucket, 12½". The dark stains inside suggest its use to serve "long sweetening," the syrup that was as black as molasses. Collection of Mr. and Mrs. John Black, New York. Photograph: Black.*

*36. BOOTE'S 1851 OCTAGON SHAPE hot beverage jug is uncommon in that there is no hole for ventilation and the cover is elliptical on one side. Lucky owners are John and Jane Yunginger, Minnesota. Photograph: Blair.*

*37. GRAPE OCTAGON miniature, SYDENHAM-type tea set potted by Clementson displayed beside standard teapot in Boote's 1851 OCTAGON SHAPE with ringed handle. From the collection of Mr. and Mrs. James Walker. Photograph: Blair.*

# IX  Famous Names

In 1850, Wedgwood & Co. marketed white ironstone dishes labeled *Erie Shape*, and Barrow & Co. also registered their *Adriatic Shape* at that time. The only piece of *Erie Shape* I have seen was a plain platter with no raised decoration. Perhaps the finials were decorative and original enough to warrant this special mark.

These two patterns, closely followed by the popular Boote's *Sydenham Shape* in 1853, were the first examples of the practice among Staffordshire potters of naming some white ironstone patterns after well-known people or places.

T. & R. Boote followed their big success with such patterns as *Grenade Shape*, *Union Shape*, *Chinese Shape* and the several forms of *Atlantic Shape*. Most Boote dishes that remain are still unchecked and unstained today.

John Alcock shaped the *Paris*, *Trent* and *Stafford* patterns. Joseph Clementson contributed during these years with his *LaFayette Shape, New York Shape,* and he also made the *Chinese Shape*.

In this book, I have no drawings or photographs for the 1855 pattern by Alcock, *Stafford Shape;* for the octagonal *Montpelier Shape;* or for *Kansas Shape*. However, I have seen them!

These familiar names on the shapes of white ironstone helped the consumers to name their desires as they placed their orders with the Staffordshire potteries. Naturally, New Yorkers were eager to purchase a pattern named after their special state, etc. The connotations were flattering and helped maintain interest in new offerings from china merchants.

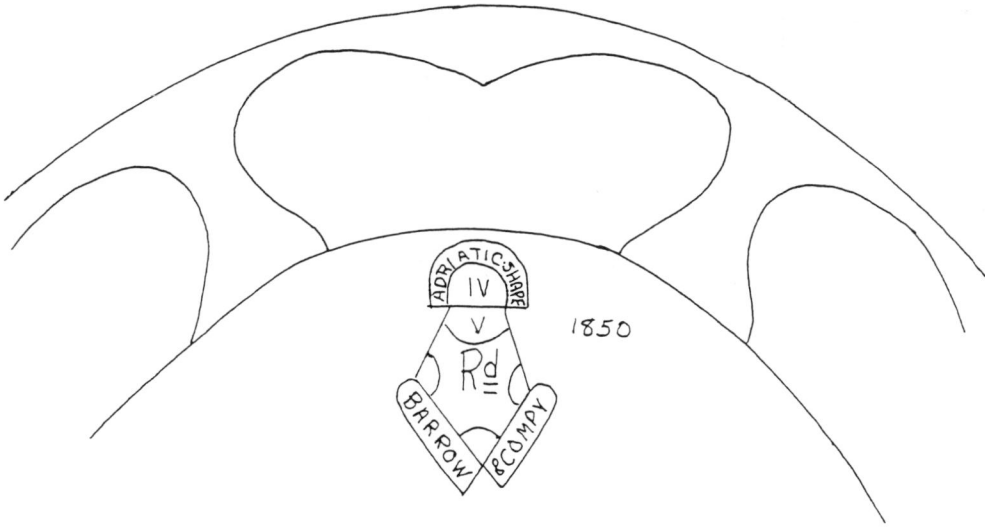

**Adriatic Shape** Barrow & Co. registered 1850.

**De Soto Shape** Thos. Hughes, registered 1855.

**Grenade Shape** T. & R. Boote. This pattern includes an unusual one-cup teapot. See Photograph 38.

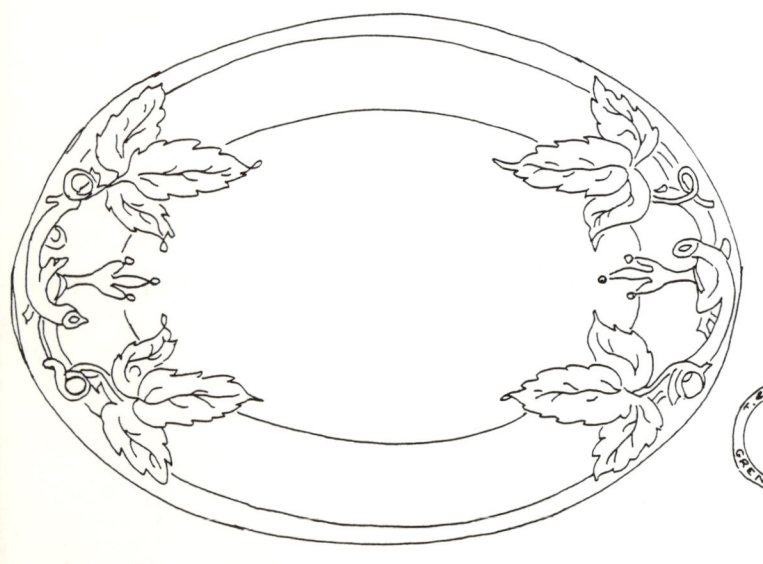

*38 A Berlin sugar bowl by Liddle, Elliott & Son shows the size of the rare, one-cup GRENADE teapot potted by T.&R. Boote. Note the same handle details as found in CHINESE SHAPE. Photograph: Blair.*

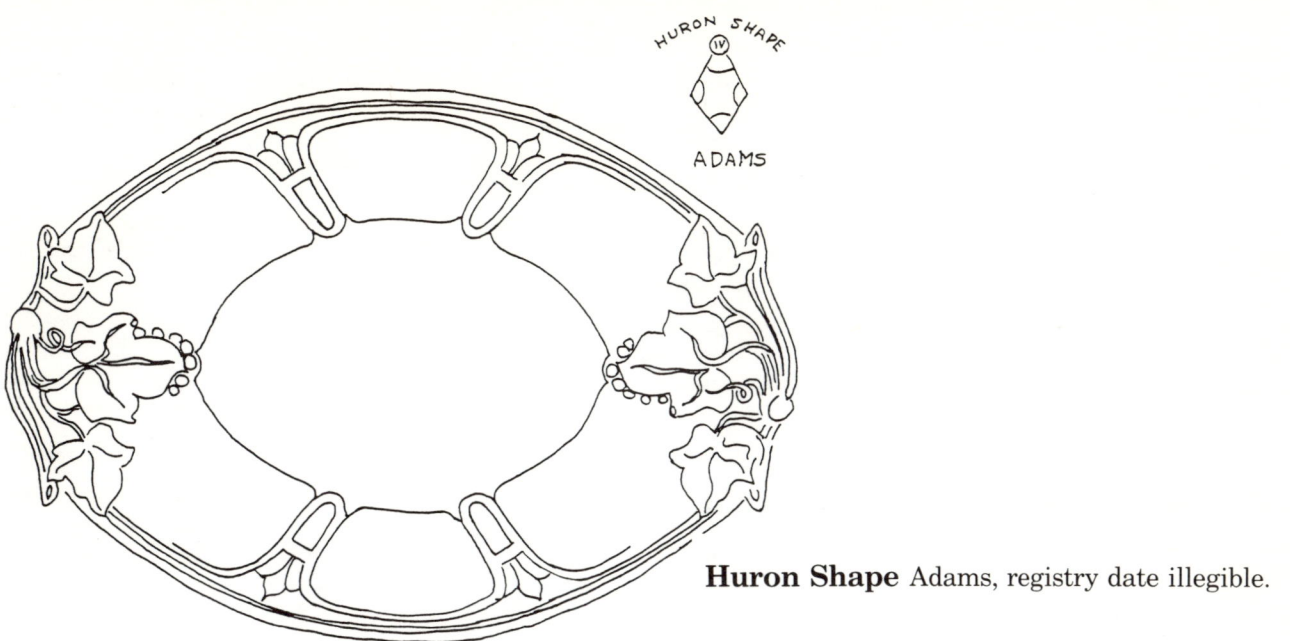

**Huron Shape** Adams, registry date illegible.

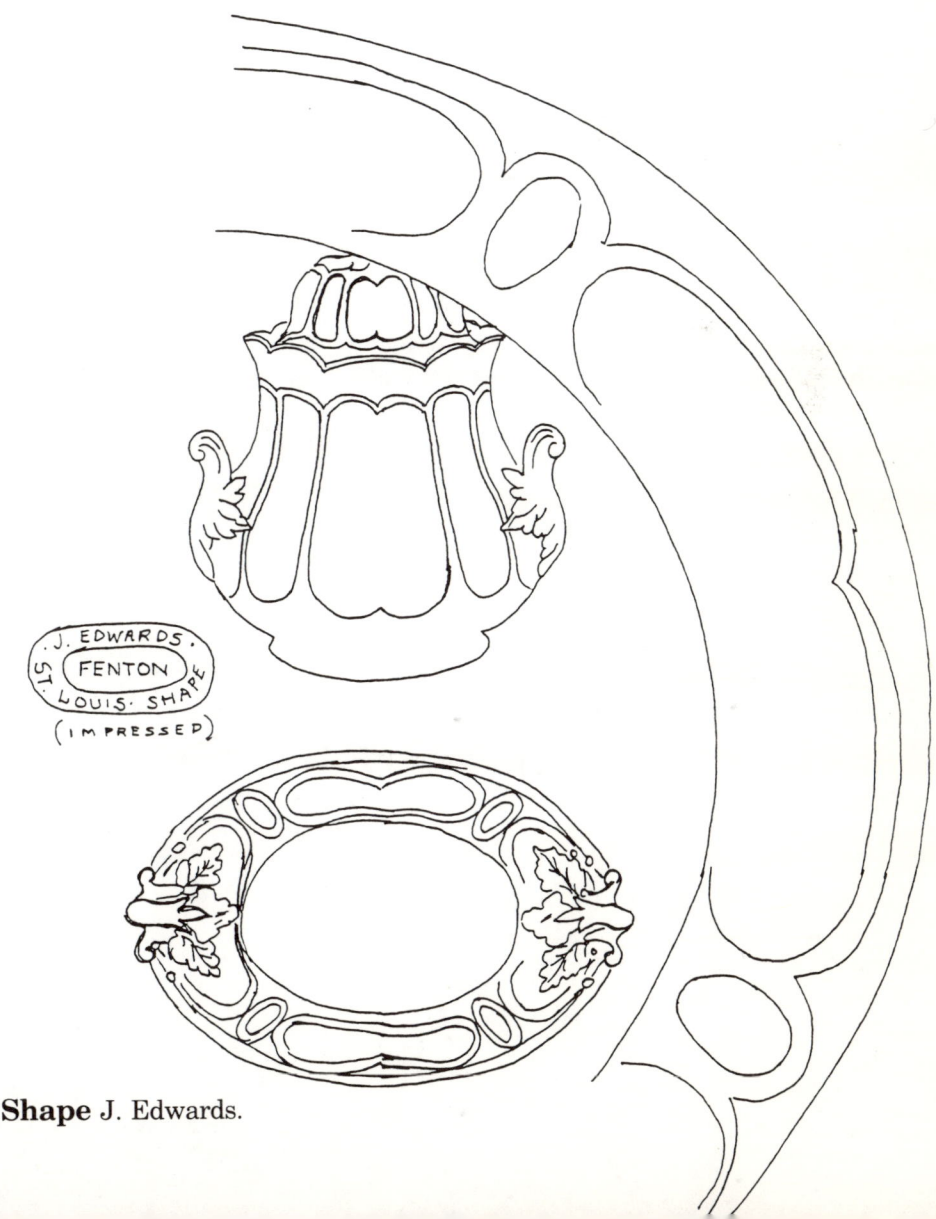

**St. Louis Shape** J. Edwards.

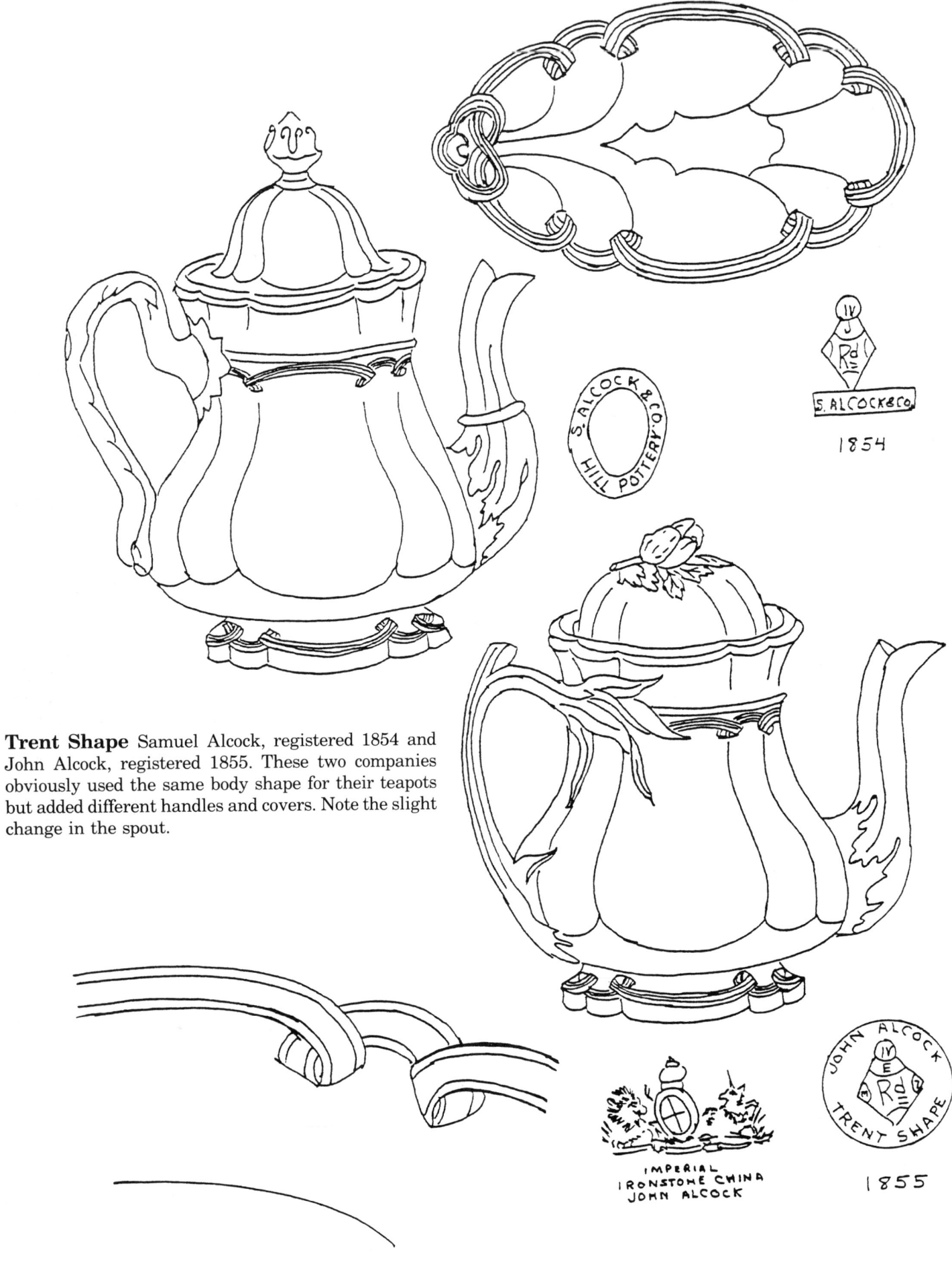

**Trent Shape** Samuel Alcock, registered 1854 and John Alcock, registered 1855. These two companies obviously used the same body shape for their teapots but added different handles and covers. Note the slight change in the spout.

**Union Shape** T. & R. Boote. 9¾" high, registered 1856.

*39. UNION SHAPE pitcher by T. & R. Boote. Collection of Mr. and Mrs. William Horner. Photograph: Dr. Horner.*

**LaFayette Shape**

J. Clementson, circa early 1850s.

**Virginia Shape** Brougham & Mayer, registered 1855.

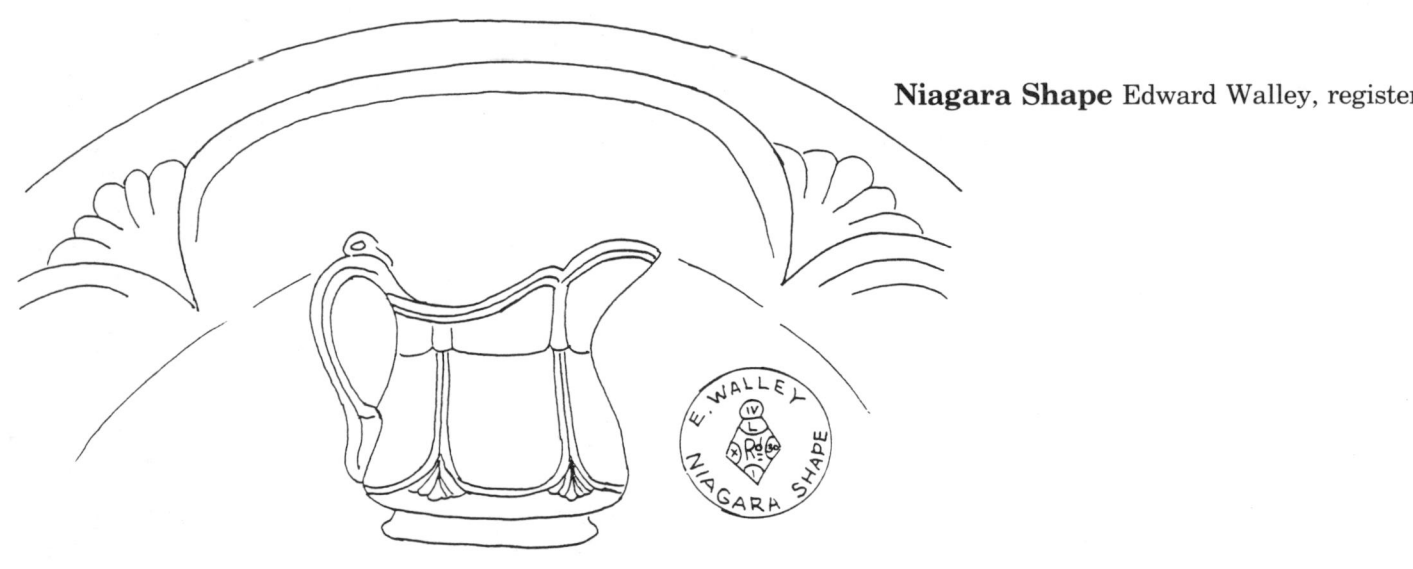

**Niagara Shape** Edward Walley, registered 1856.

**Portland Shape** Elsmore & Forster.

40. PORTLAND SHAPE by Elsmore & Forster. The remarkable bellflower finials are a fascination to collectors. Collection of James and Doris Walker, New York. Photograph: Blair.

**Girard Shape** J. Ridgway Bates.

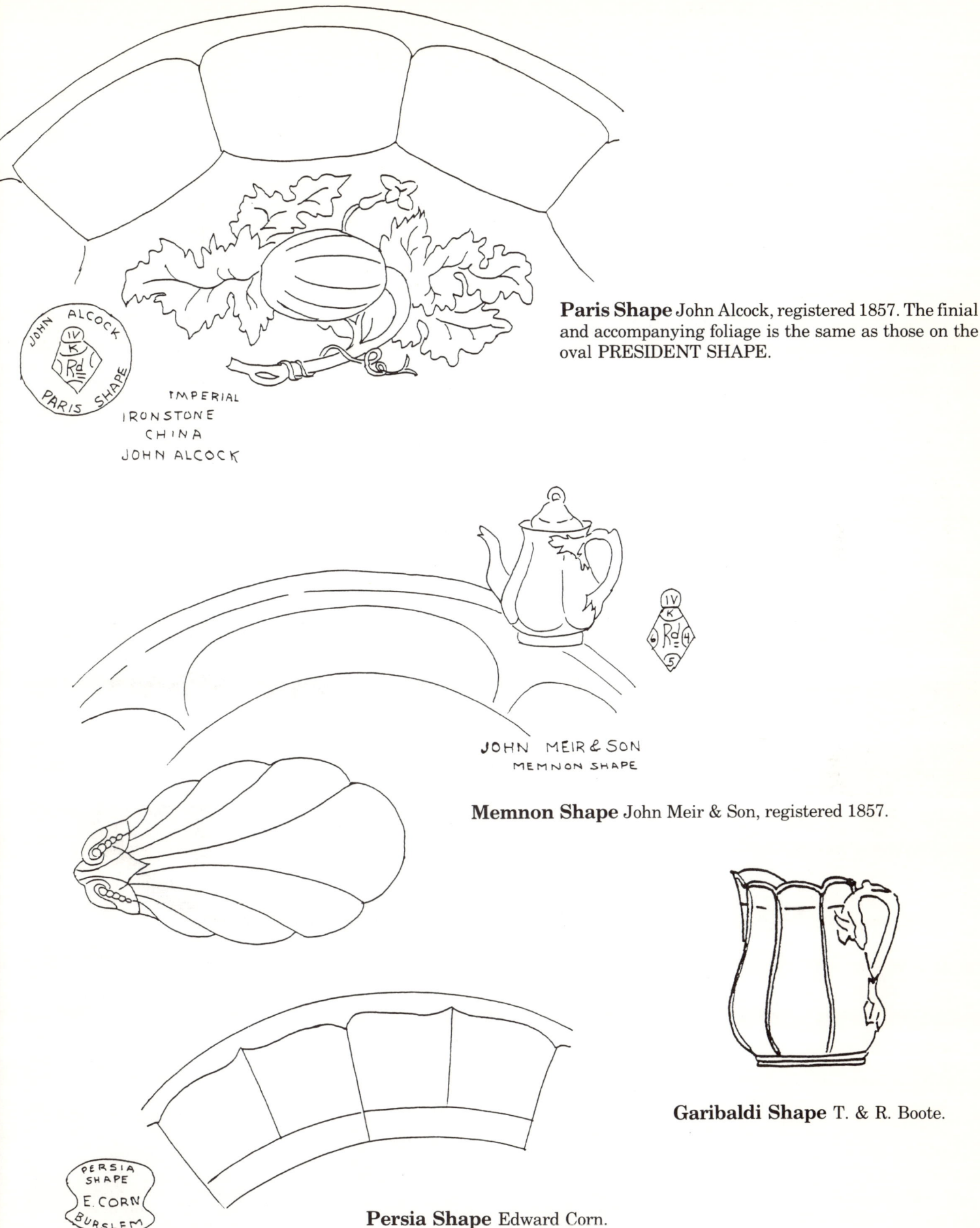

**Paris Shape** John Alcock, registered 1857. The finial and accompanying foliage is the same as those on the oval PRESIDENT SHAPE.

**Memnon Shape** John Meir & Son, registered 1857.

**Garibaldi Shape** T. & R. Boote.

**Persia Shape** Edward Corn.

**New York Shape** J. Clementson, registered 1858. The alternate finial is drawn below to the right. To the right above are details of the handles and plate designs. (See Photographs 41, 42.)

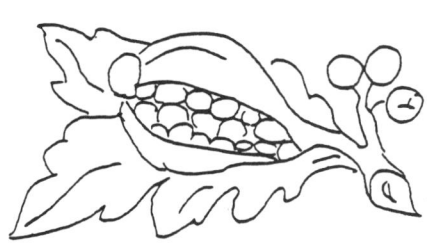

*41. NEW YORK SHAPE shaving mug and horizontal toothbrush holder from a toilet set by J. Clementson. Photograph: Blair.*

*42. NEW YORK SHAPE tea set main pieces. Photograph: Blair.*

**Chinese Shape** J. Clementson, also T. & R. Boote and Anthony Shaw.

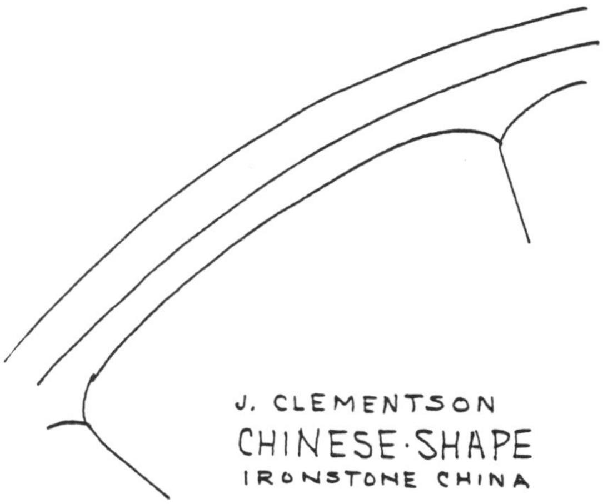

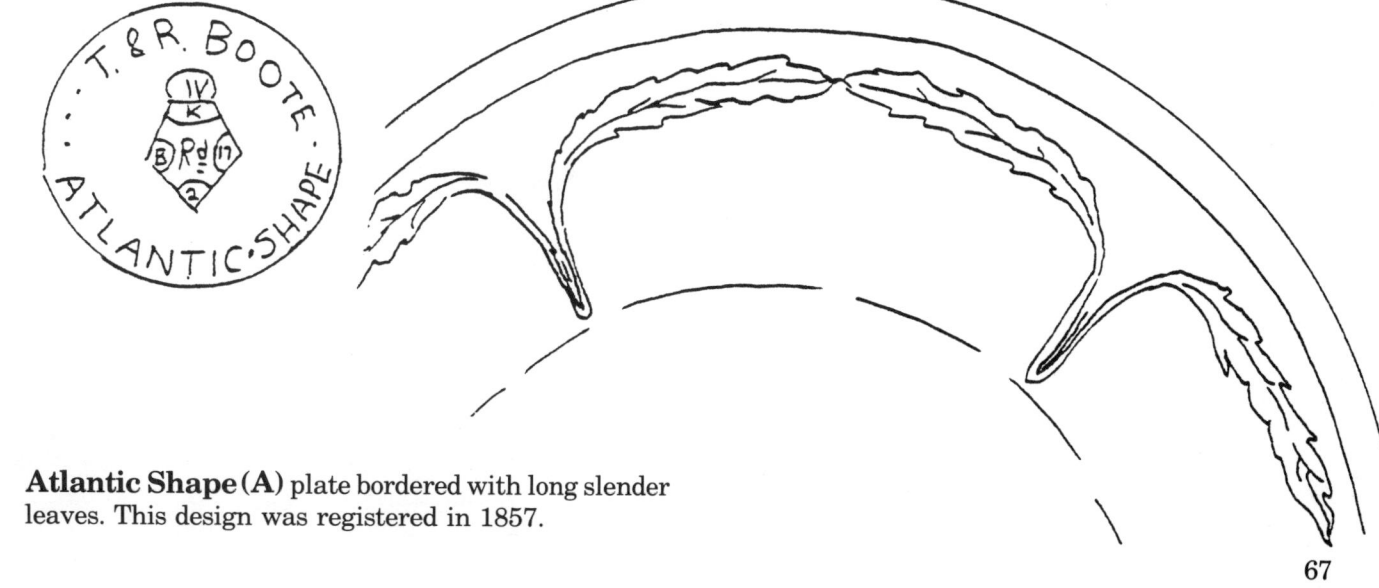

43. CHINESE SHAPE by T. & R. Boote. Pieces located by Tom Needham, Kansas. Photograph: Blair.

Unmarked. T. & R. Boote design

**Atlantic Shape (A)** plate bordered with long slender leaves. This design was registered in 1857.

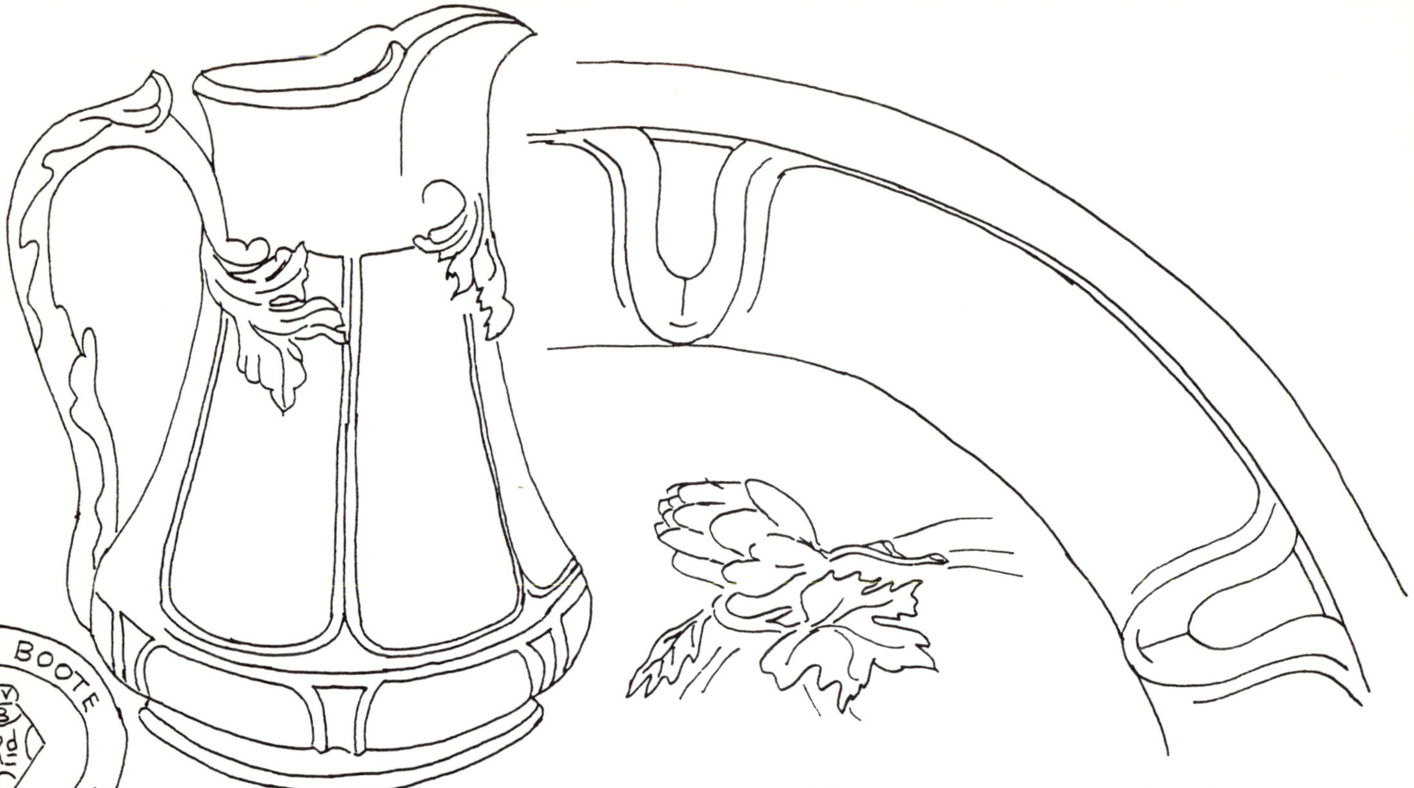

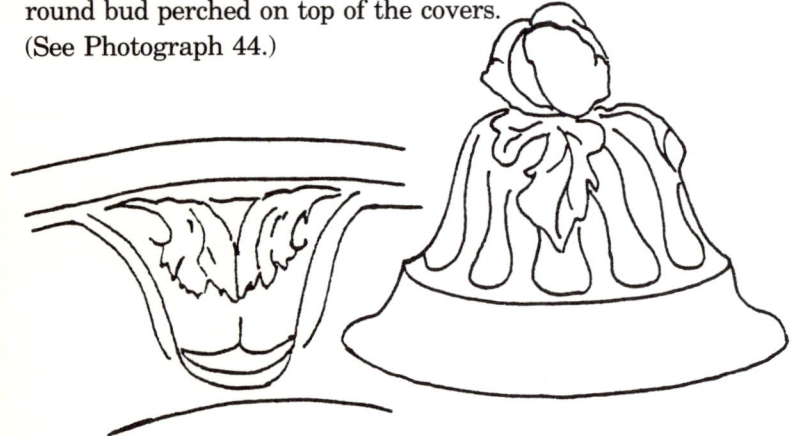

**Atlantic Shape (B)** T. & R. Boote, registered 1858. This shape had heavy lines covering the base of the pitchers and teapots. This same decor covered the fullest part of the body of the covered dishes. The finial was a large artichoke.

**Atlantic Shape (C)** T. & R. Boote, registered 1858. The base of the beverage servers were ringed with large thumbprints. The plate motifs had added foliage. A round bud perched on top of the covers. (See Photograph 44.)

44. ATLANTIC SHAPE (C) by Boote. This used the same handle and leaves under the spout as the B shape but the spout was squared, the base had large thumbprints, and the finial was formed as a bud. Collection of James and Doris Walker. Photograph: Blair.

# X  Golden Waves of Grain

The word "ironstone" often brings to mind that most famous of old white china, a wheat design. This fact was driven home most forcibly by Norman Rockwell, the great American illustrator of the Common Man. He chose a scene called *FREEDOM FROM WANT* for use in one of his Four Freedom series. A middle-class American family is gathered happily and hungrily around the laden table set with plain ironstone on spotless linen. Grandpa hovers over Grandma as she proudly bears the crispy, brown turkey on the traditional enormous ironstone platter. In the foreground shines a large covered ironstone tureen, blue-white, with melon shaped ribs and borders of heavily embossed wheat heads and stalks. This well-publicized wheat pattern has grown to symbolize the fruitfulness of our farms.

*45. WHEAT patterned dishes. Photograph: LeBel.*

Collectors have been especially fascinated by the *CORN AND OATS* pattern which is particularly adapted to the round and oval shapes. The grains are deeply impressed, every piece being bordered.

**Corn and Oats** Davenport, also J. Wedgwood, registered 1863.

*46. CORN AND OATS, a favorite pattern, potted by both J. Wedgwood and Davenport. Pitcher is owned by Jean Hogg, New York, and the other pieces by the Wetherbees. Photograph: Blair.*

*Wheat and Blackberry* is truly a beautiful composition molded by J. & G. Meakin about 1865. The clusters of berries, grain, and tapering stalks give an effect of almost having been carved. Jacob Furnival initiated a similar pattern about 1860. W. Taylor, Robert Cochran, and St. Johns Chinaware Co. used the design.

A design marked *Pearl* has been often called *Wheat and Clover*. The decorations are related to other wheat patterns but are elaborated by a ribbon bow and clover leaves with blossoms amid the usual wheat. At least four potters popularized the wheat and clover motif.

*47. CERES SHAPE by Elsmore & Forster, best known white ironstone pattern through the years. Oval tureen, 16½", complete with cracker tray and ladle. Owners are Mr. and Mrs. John Black. Photograph: Black.*

*48. CERES SHAPE teapot and plate with scalloped edge. Melon ribs characterize many of the wheat patterns. Photograph: Blair.*

The "most wanted" wheat pattern was named *Ceres* in honor of the Roman goddess of agriculture. This shape was registered by Elsmore & Forster, Tunstall in 1859, and continued in production later by Turner, Goddard & Co. A detail of the motif shows three rows of wheat grains in each head among graceful leaf stalks and includes a twisted rope band circling the bases and the necks.

Other more common table services simply called the *Wheat* pattern have twelve vertical melon-shaped ribs on the bowls and pitchers and a scalloped border deep inside the flatware. This most common *Wheat* form is topped with finials in the shape of an open sheaf resting on wheat heads and foliage. Among the manufacturers were Turner, Goddard & Co., Turner & Tomkinson, Elsmore & Forster, J. & G. Meakin, Wilkinson, and W. & E. Corn, 1870. No rope band is included.

A similar pattern is tagged *Wheat, Bulbous Shape* and has the same general decor as the above. However, the ribs taper slightly at the neck and the effect is rather clumsy. Turner & Goddard and W. & E. Corn produced this not-so-popular design in the 1870s. J. F. potted a pear-shaped sugar bowl with no ribs on the side. Instead, stalks of wheat and shards arch out from the handles.

**Ceres Shape** originated by Elsmore & Forster in 1859, subsequently produced by Turner, Goddard & Co. and E. Pearson. (See Photographs 47, 48, 49.)

49. *CERES miniature tea set by Elsmore & Forster (rare, clearly marked). Owners are John and Jane Yunginger from Minnesota. Photograph: Blair.*

We can also mention an example nicknamed *Wheat and Poppy* which is also stamped *Prairie Shape*. This wheat pattern does not make use of the usual melon-shaped ribs or the wheat border. It can often be confused with a similar pattern nicknamed *Prairie Flowers*. The "wheat" heads in this second decoration have long beards. The field grasses, clover and flowers impressed on these dishes are clear, sharp, and very detailed. The *Prairie Shape* was potted by both Livesley & Powell and Joseph Clementson, registered in 1862, while *Prairie Flowers* was introduced by such experts as Livesley & Powell in 1862, and their successors, Powell & Bishop, circa 1876. *Scotia Shape* from the kilns of F. Jones & Co., Longton, circa 1870, is bordered with wheat and poppies and has convex ribs.

The common wheat motif has been continuously reproduced. By the turn of the century the designs were quite vague and the color a creamy white rather than the blued-white employed by the early Staffordshire potteries. Today, several companies both in England and the United States reproduce this white ironstone design.

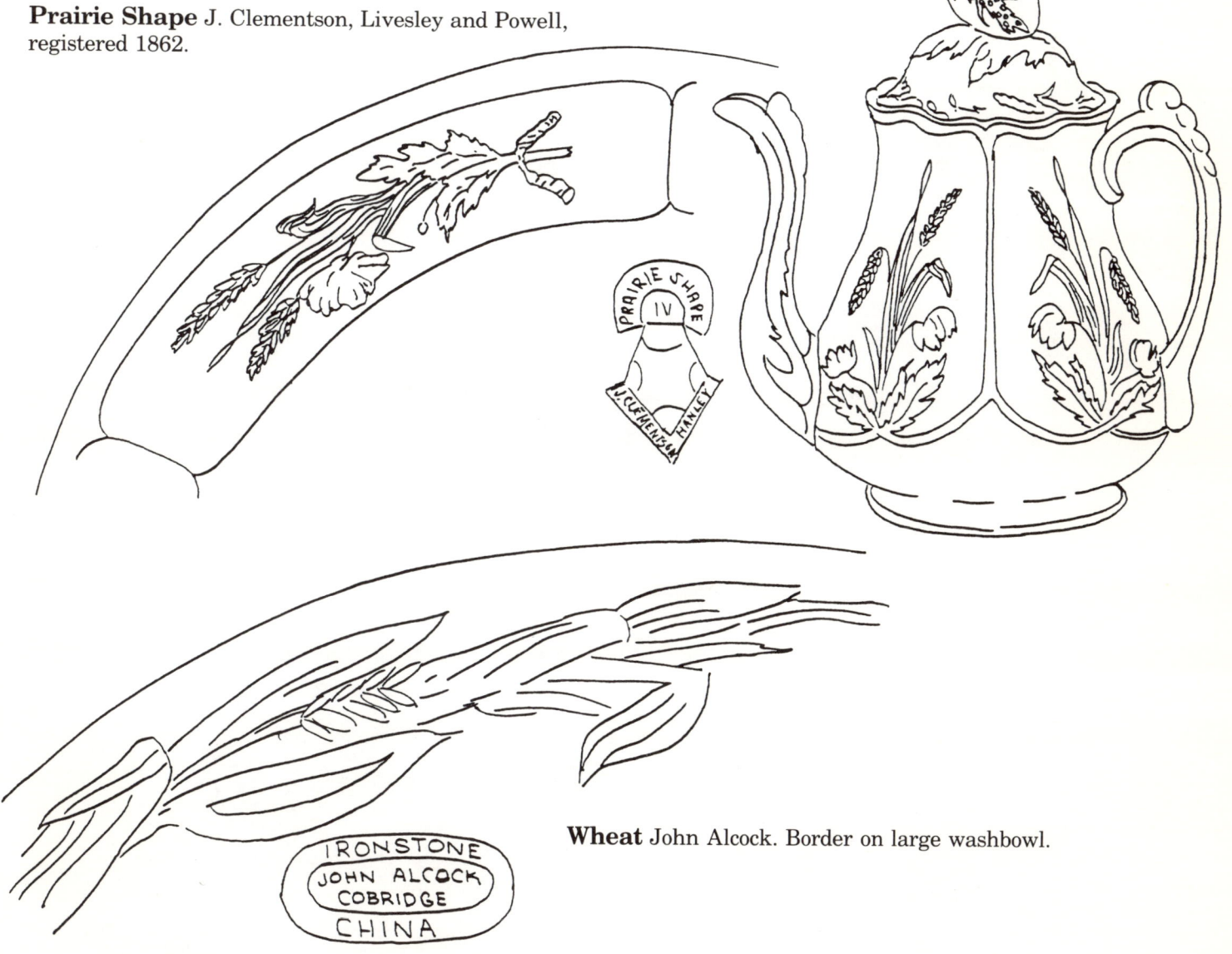

**Prairie Shape** J. Clementson, Livesley and Powell, registered 1862.

**Wheat** John Alcock. Border on large washbowl.

**Prairie Flowers** Livesley & Powell, Powell & Bishop.

**Have —— Shape** (name illegible) Holland and Green.

(See Photograph 50.)

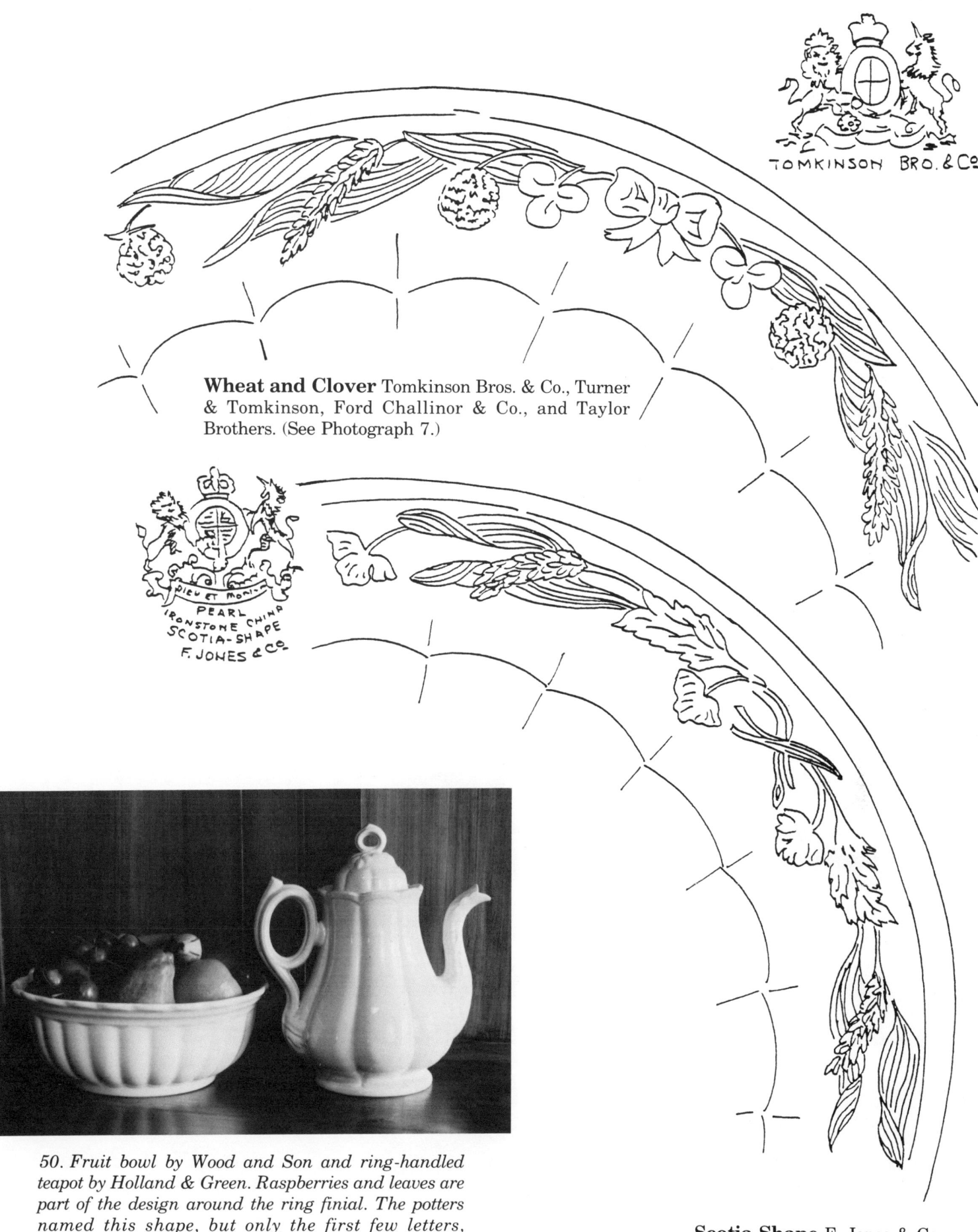

**Wheat and Clover** Tomkinson Bros. & Co., Turner & Tomkinson, Ford Challinor & Co., and Taylor Brothers. (See Photograph 7.)

50. Fruit bowl by Wood and Son and ring-handled teapot by Holland & Green. Raspberries and leaves are part of the design around the ring finial. The potters named this shape, but only the first few letters, HAVE——, can be read. Photograph: Blair.

**Scotia Shape** F. Jones & Co.

**Wheat and Blackberry** J. & G. Meakin, J. F., W. Taylor, Robert Cochran & Co. and also an American pottery company, St. Johns Chinaware Co. in Canada.

51. WHEAT AND BLACKBERRY ewer and basin by J. & G. Meakin with deeply sculptured berries and leaves. Owned by Warren and Christie Wetherbee. Photograph: Blair.

**Canada** has been attributed to Meikle Bros., Liverpool. Below, right, are two marks found on soup tureens in this pattern.

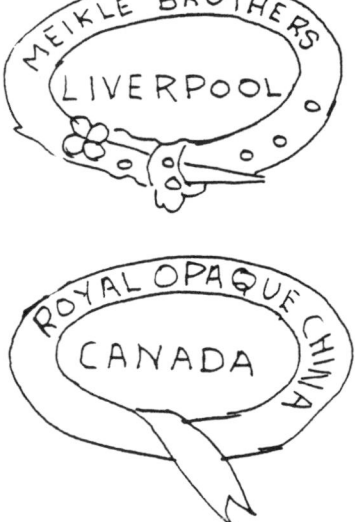

52. CANADA wheat and poppy design registered in 1877. No potter's mark on soup tureen. Owned by James and Doris Walker, New York. Photograph: Blair.

**Wheat with Flowers** Bishop & Stonier. This is one of the later wheat patterns repeated three times around a soup plate border.

**Wheat in the Meadow** Powell & Bishop, registered 1869.

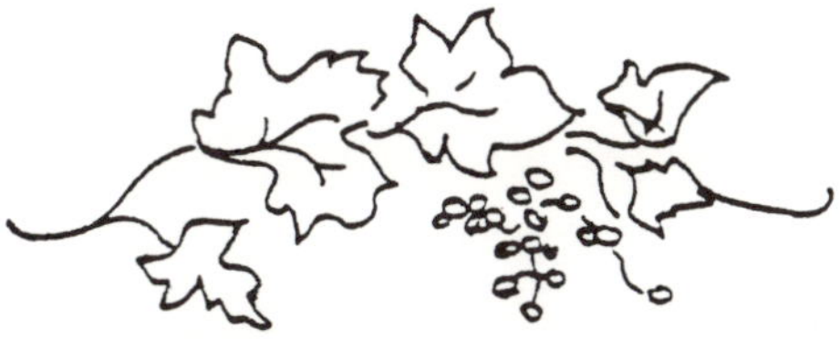

**Wheat and Grape** unmarked. This decor, a cluster of grapes with leaves, was copied from a wheat-bordered compote.

# XI  Green of the Earth

*I went down into the garden of nuts to see the fruits of the valley, and to see whether the vine flourished, and the pomegranates budded.*
                                        Song of Solomon

Designers of white ironstone during the 1860s drew heavily from the gardens and woods for their designs. Nut, fruit, gourd, cone, and acorn finials were often used in realistic forms.

A few of these leaf-decorated shapes were named but seldom were dated. Grape, oak, ivy, holly, and berry leaves were most often wrapped around handles and spouts. Blackberry and grape clusters were hidden in the foliage very much as they are in our gardens today.

In this way, the alert potters appealed to the love of husbandry in the heart of American consumers.

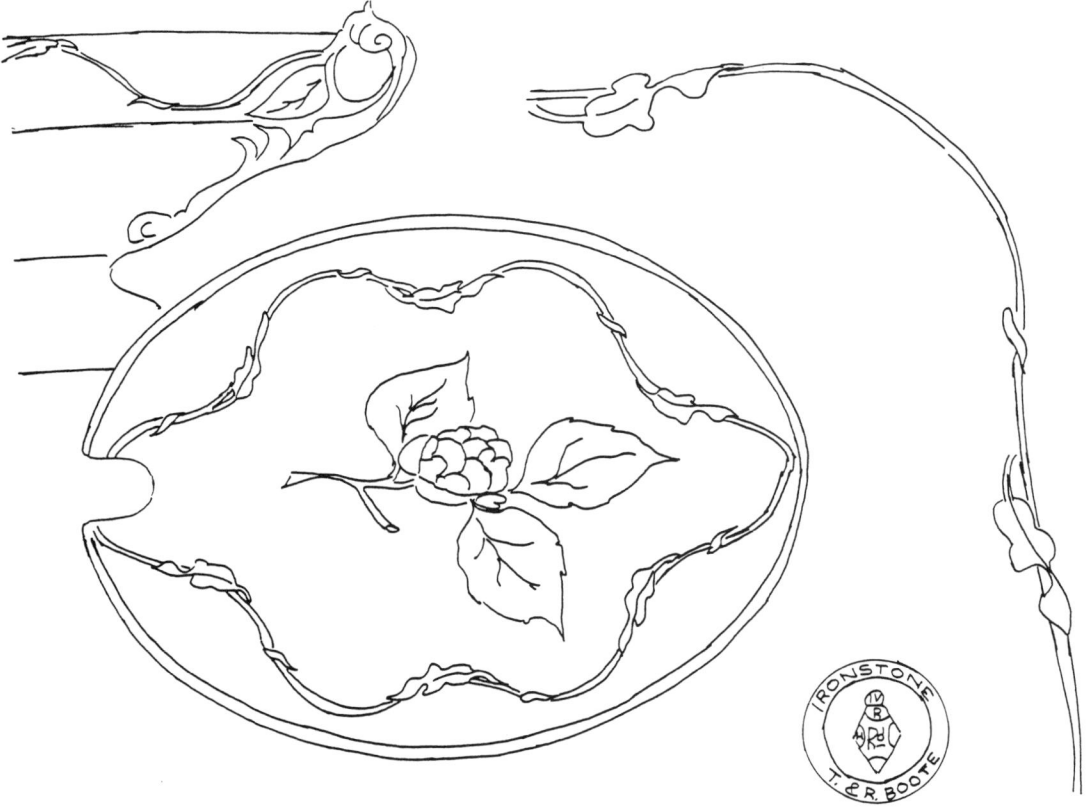

**Winding Vine** T. & R. Boote, registered 1861.

78

**Sharon Arch** Davenport, also J. Wedgwood. 9½" soup bowl, registered 1861. Gravy boat, unmarked.

53. SHARON ARCH patterned dishes potted by both Davenport and J. Wedgwood are unusually heavy. Dinner plate weighs two pounds; ring-handled pitcher, four pounds; covered vegetable dish, three pounds. Handleless cup is pictured, but handled version was also made. Photograph: Blair.

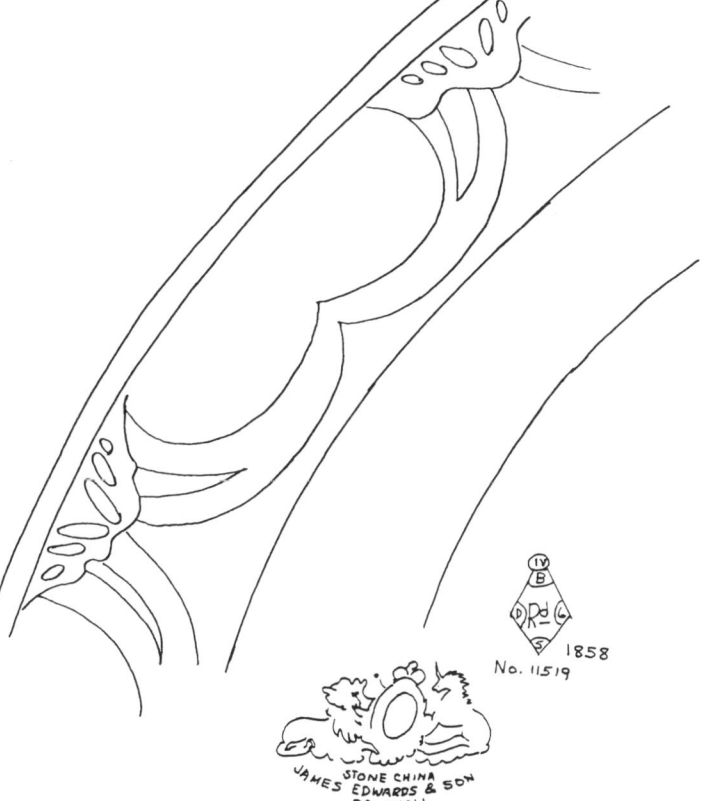

54. HANGING ARCH pattern included twig handles and finial with surrounding fruit and leaves by James Edwards & Son. Collection of James and Doris Walker. Photograph: Blair.

**Hanging Arch** James Edwards & Son. Platter 16½" long.

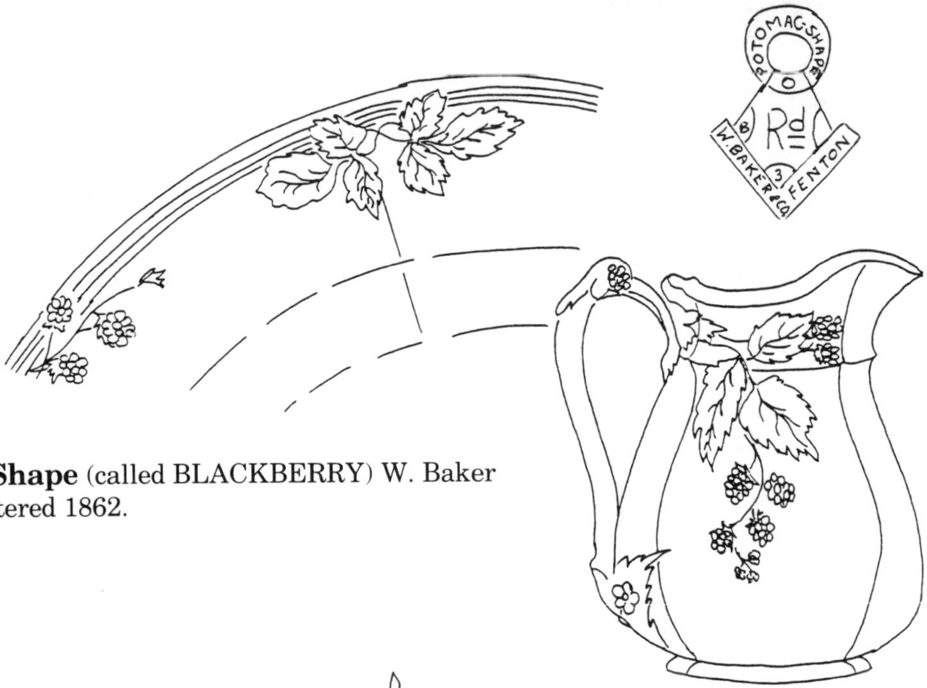

**Potomac Shape** (called BLACKBERRY) W. Baker & Co., registered 1862.

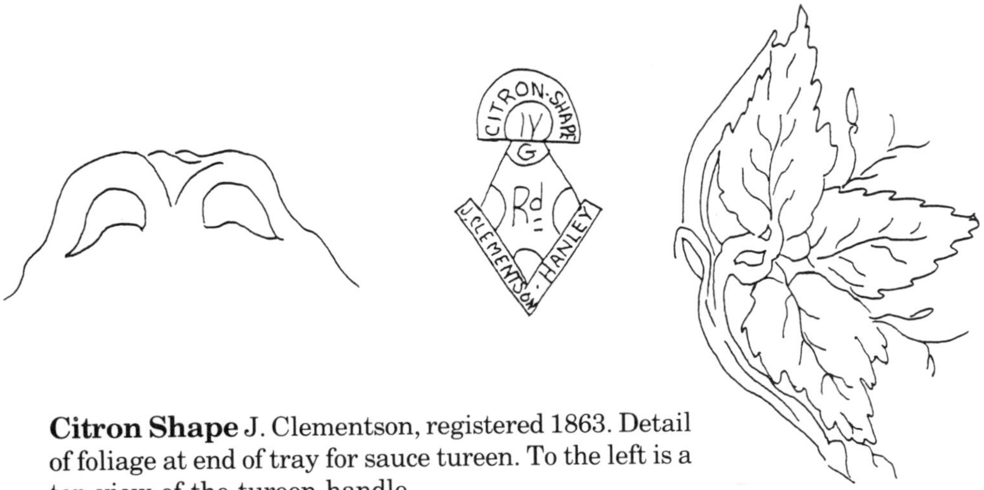

**Citron Shape** J. Clementson, registered 1863. Detail of foliage at end of tray for sauce tureen. To the left is a top view of the tureen handle.

**Acorn** Unmarked.

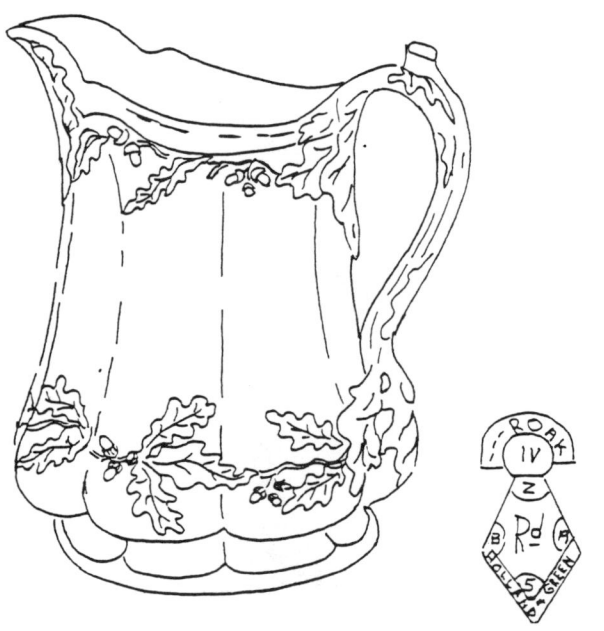

**White Oak and Acorn** Holland & Green. This pattern was named but the letters were blurred on this beautiful pitcher.

**Tiny Oak and Acorn** J. W. Pankhurst. The oval tureen measures 12″ long.

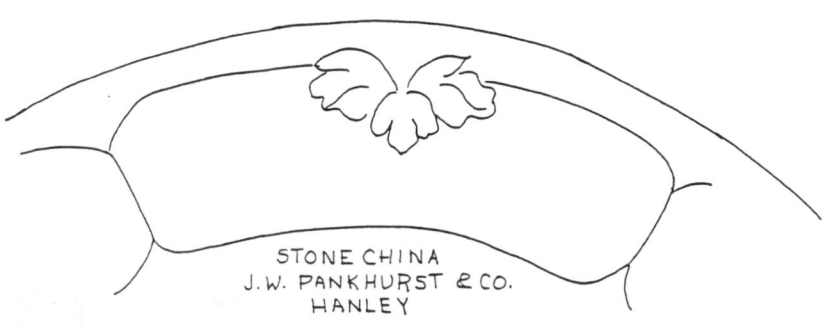

**Framed Leaf** J. W. Pankhurst & Co.

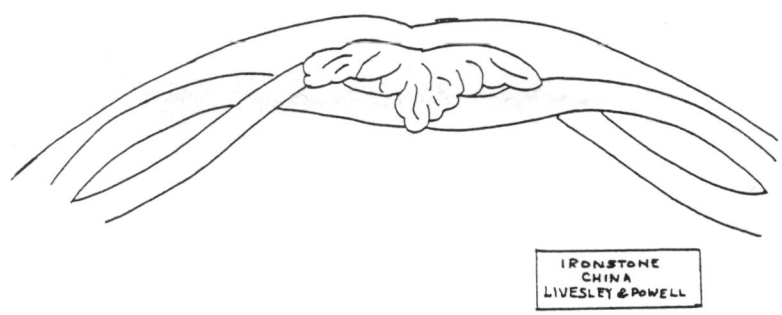
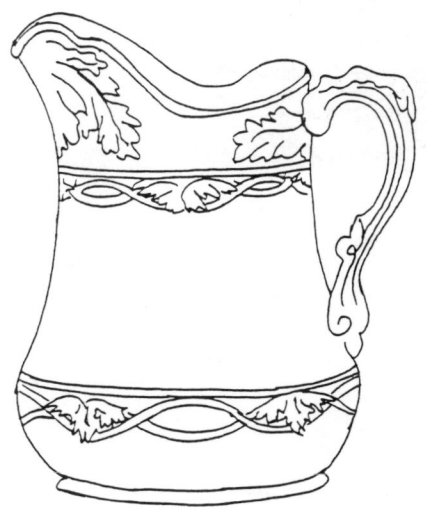

**Leaf and Crossed Ribbon** Livesley & Powell.

81

**Draped Leaf (A)** J. Clementson. The name of this shape is illegible.

**Draped Leaf (B)** James Edwards.

**Draped Leaf (C)** Bridgwood & Clarke. Heavy bodied, three-quart pitcher.

**Draped Leaf (D)** Henry Alcock & Co.

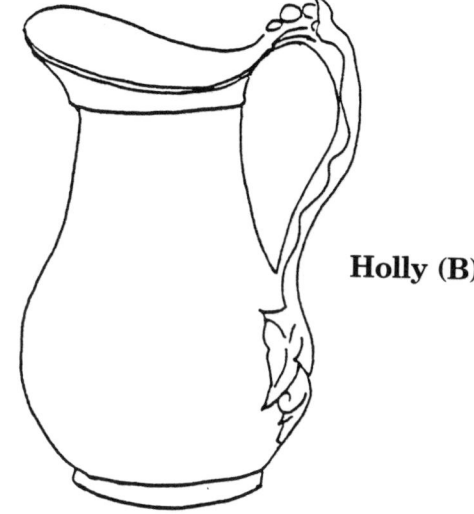

**Holly (B)**

**Holly (A)**

**Holly** Maddock (& Son). Here are three variations of this pattern. All employ holly berries and the same leaf wrapped around the handles of the pitchers. Notice similar decor on GRENADE SHAPE and CHINESE SHAPE pitchers. CHINESE SHAPE also portrays the body decoration used on HOLLY (A).

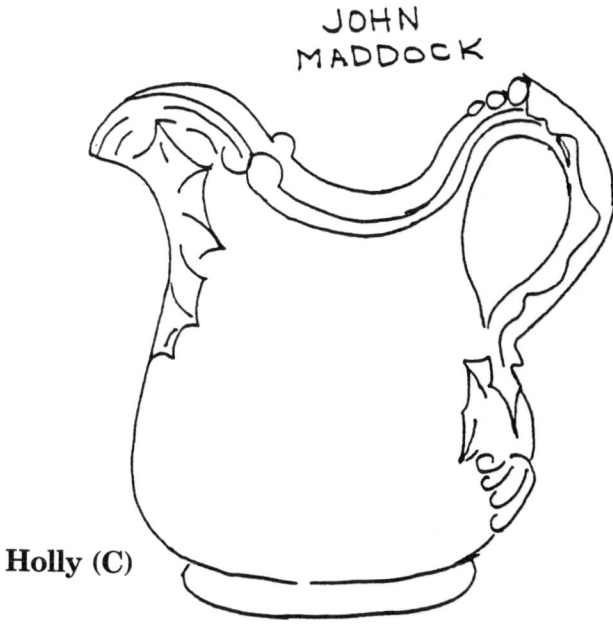

**Holly (C)**

55. *HOLLY pitchers in three sizes by Maddock. From the collections of three New York families: the Pecoras, the Hoggs, and the Wetherbees. Photograph: Blair.*

**Vintage Shape** Adams, later repeated more extensively by E. & C. Challinor, circa 1865. It has been nicknamed GRAPE AND MEDALLION.

**Gooseberry** Marked W. G. (?).

**Arbor Vine** Wedgwood & Co.

ROYAL STONE CHINA
WEDGWOOD & CO.

STONE GRANITE
(impressed)

**Loop and Dot** E. & C. Challinor after 1862.

**Winterberry** Unmarked.

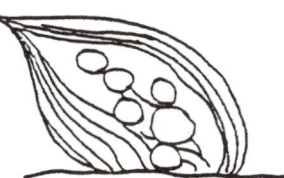

56. WINTERBERRY *pattern toothbrush holder with ventilating hole, not marked in potting. Photograph: Blair.*

57. POMEGRANATE *by J. F. uses the same finial and foliage as Clementson's COLUMBIA SHAPE and Boote's CHINESE. Borders are the same as TRENT SHAPE. Collection of James and Doris Walker, New York. Photograph: Blair.*

**Cone with Leaves** James Edwards. This finial was much used: on this pattern, on WASHINGTON SHAPE, and on some vegetable servers in the pattern named HYACINTH.

**Double Groove** Marked J. F.

**Panelled Grape** Marked J. F. Also used by Edward Pearson.

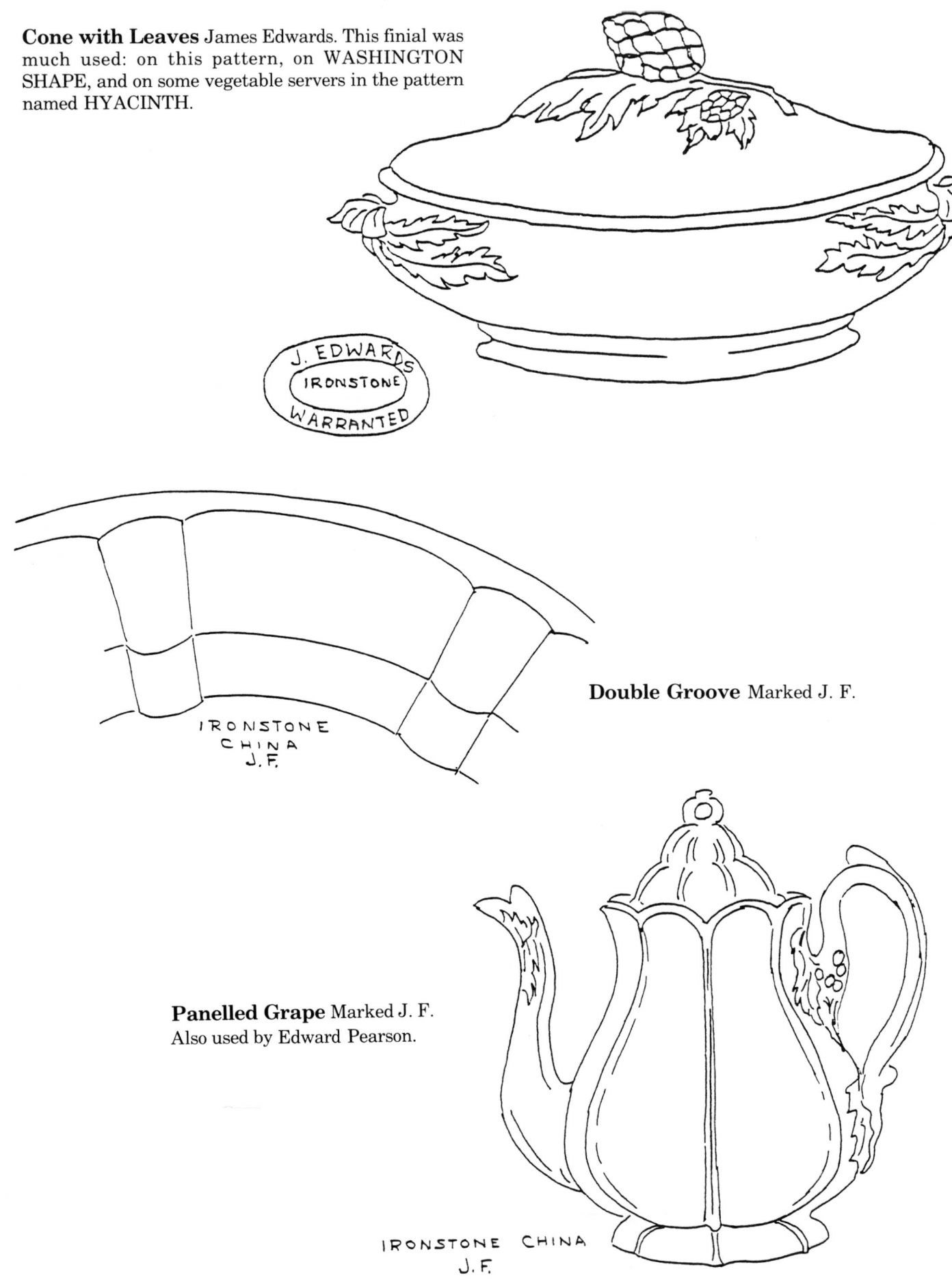

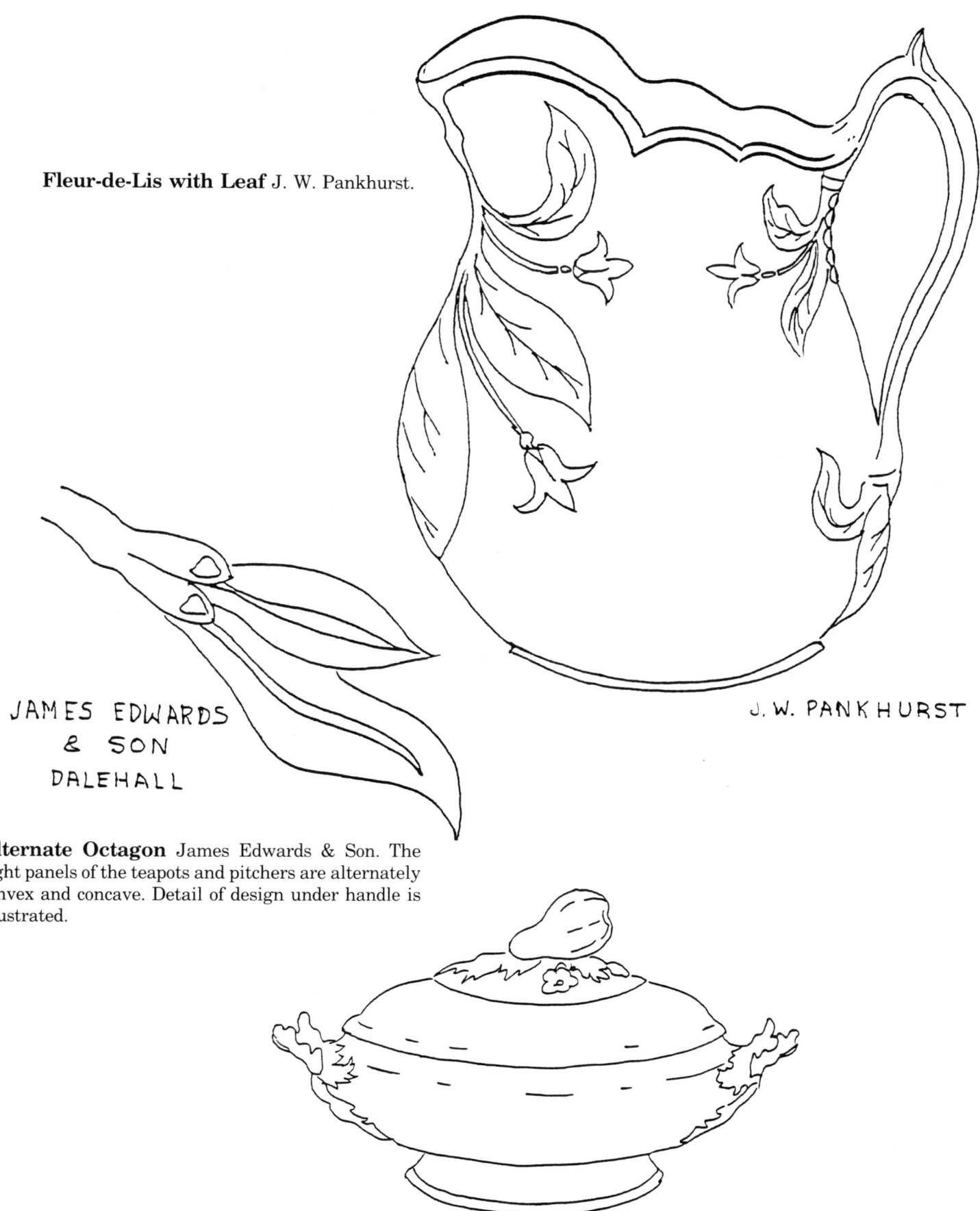

**Fleur-de-Lis with Leaf** J. W. Pankhurst.

**Alternate Octagon** James Edwards & Son. The eight panels of the teapots and pitchers are alternately convex and concave. Detail of design under handle is illustrated.

**Gourd** James Edwards & Son.

**Lily Pad** J. W. Pankhurst. This unusual, profusely decorated pattern was used on plates, a high pedestaled compote, and a three-legged cookie plate.

*58. LILY PAD design, three-legged cookie plate by J. W. Pankhurst. This design was also potted in a taller pedestaled compote. Photograph: Blair.*

**Scrolled Border** Bridgwood & Son.

**Shaw's Spray** Anthony Shaw.

**Little Scroll** Elsmore & Forster. This pattern includes a large oval sugar bowl with a rosebud finial.

**Nut with Bud** John Meir & Son. Notice the same nut finial on LEAF FAN by Bridgwood & Clarke.

**Ivy Wreath** John Meir, registered 1857. The ivy leaves twine around the edge of tureen covers. The lower part of the body of water pitchers is circled by a wide band of these leaves. The neck is also wreathed.

*59. LEAF FAN made by Bridgwood & Clarke has a fan of leaves under the handle. Photograph: Blair.*

**Loop and Line** Marked J. F.

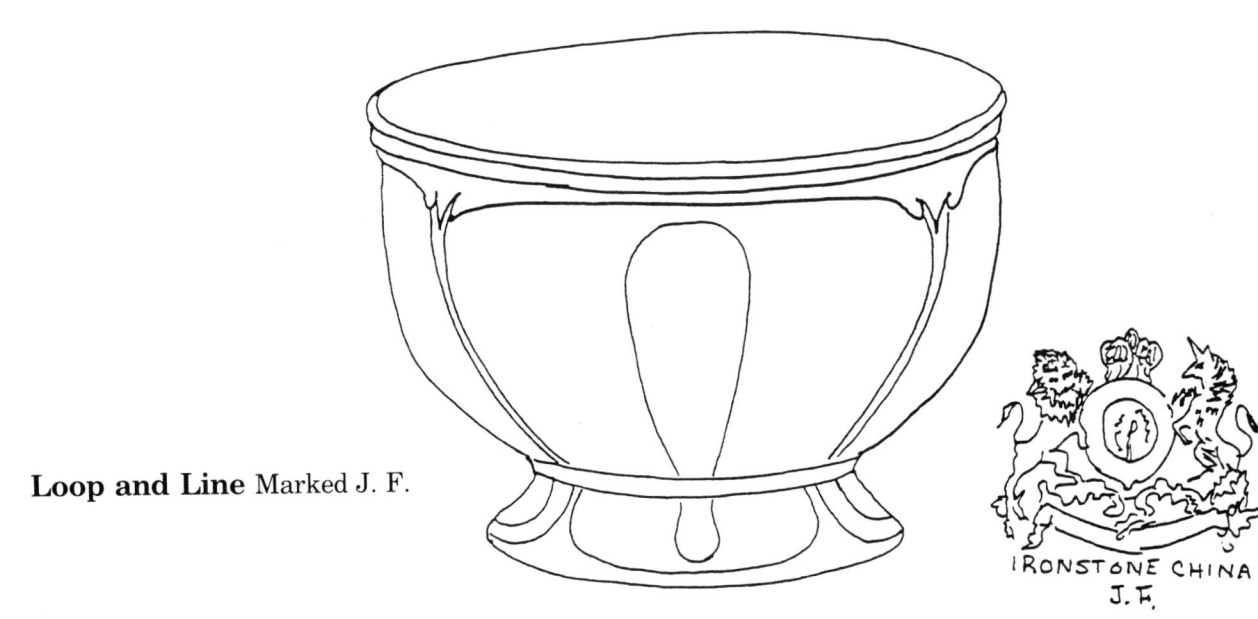

# XII   Flower Garden

Flowers from field or garden have always lifted the human heart. The Staffordshire potters looked into their own back gardens as inspiration for more ironstone patterns in the 1860s.

Long before in the 1840s James Edward had combined rosebuds with his squared shapes in *Rose Bud;* the *Chinese Shape* and one *Trent Shape* had been topped with rosebuds in the fifties and now in the sixties were introduced several wild rose motifs and the popular *Moss Rose* by J. & G. Meakin, true to detail even to the bristling stems.

We'd recognize the *Morning Glory* by Elsmore & Forster even if they had not so clearly named it. The bodies of pitchers and serving dishes are completely and clearly impressed with leaves, flowers and winding glory vines.

Another popular star in many floral motifs was the fuchsia with its graceful draping branches. We detect its drooping heads in the *Laurel* pattern, the *Fuchsia* by Jones and Meakin and *Bordered Fuchsia* by A. Shaw.

The nine patterns on pp.98-102 all include bell flowers or the shy lily of the valley drawings as copied from white ironstone dishes. The *Hyacinth* pattern, potted by Wedgwood & Co. bears little resemblance to the hyacinth that bursts up in our spring borders. The Staffordshire version is often confused with the several lily of the valley patterns and can be used easily in the same table settings. *Shaw's Lily of the Valley* can be distinguished by its bells springing from both sides of the flower stem. (This shape was later used as a base for Copper Tea Leaf trim.) The *Western* shapes had added chain borders.

The wild flowers of the prairies are found intermingled with prairie grains in the chapter on wheat.

The last pattern of this section is simply named *Fruit Garden* and includes both blooms and ripened fruit. It is unusual to find a plate in white ironstone so completely covered with design. This same pattern has been found in majolica ware.

Many a woman in a lonely spot was happy to buy china decorated with a favorite vine or flower that reminded her of happy hours or fond scenes.

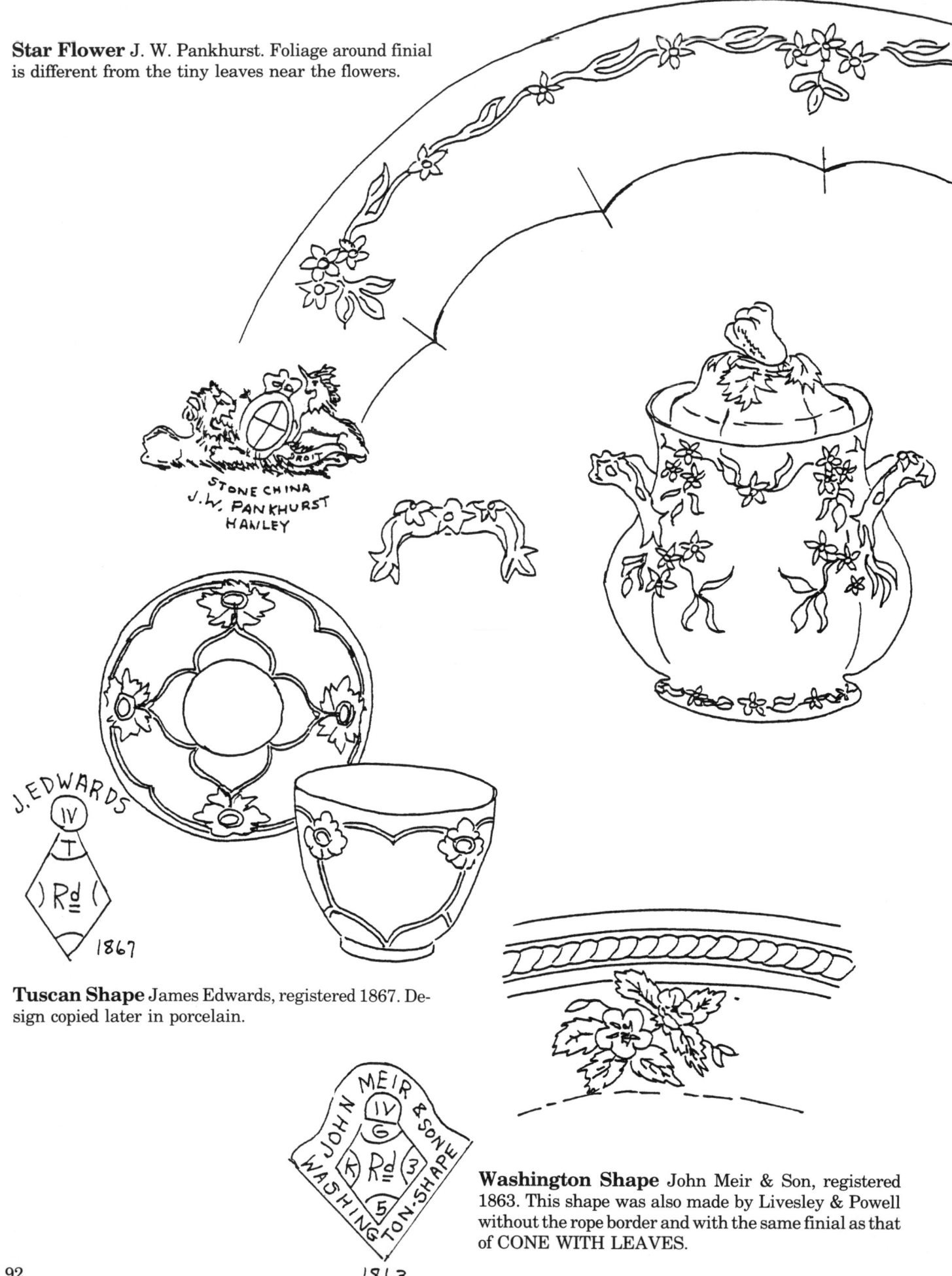

**Star Flower** J. W. Pankhurst. Foliage around finial is different from the tiny leaves near the flowers.

**Tuscan Shape** James Edwards, registered 1867. Design copied later in porcelain.

**Washington Shape** John Meir & Son, registered 1863. This shape was also made by Livesley & Powell without the rope border and with the same finial as that of CONE WITH LEAVES.

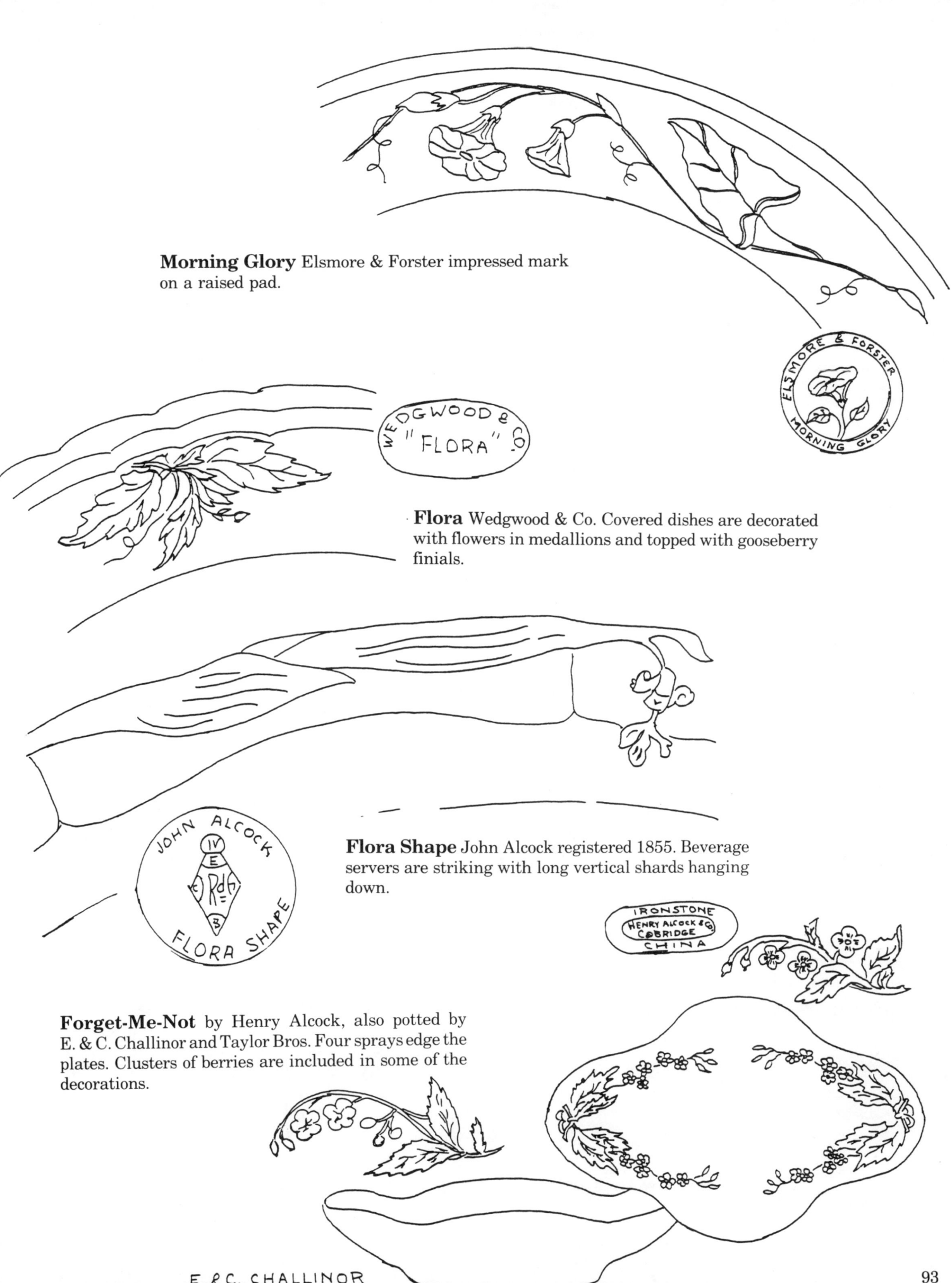

**Morning Glory** Elsmore & Forster impressed mark on a raised pad.

**Flora** Wedgwood & Co. Covered dishes are decorated with flowers in medallions and topped with gooseberry finials.

**Flora Shape** John Alcock registered 1855. Beverage servers are striking with long vertical shards hanging down.

**Forget-Me-Not** by Henry Alcock, also potted by E. & C. Challinor and Taylor Bros. Four sprays edge the plates. Clusters of berries are included in some of the decorations.

E. & C. CHALLINOR

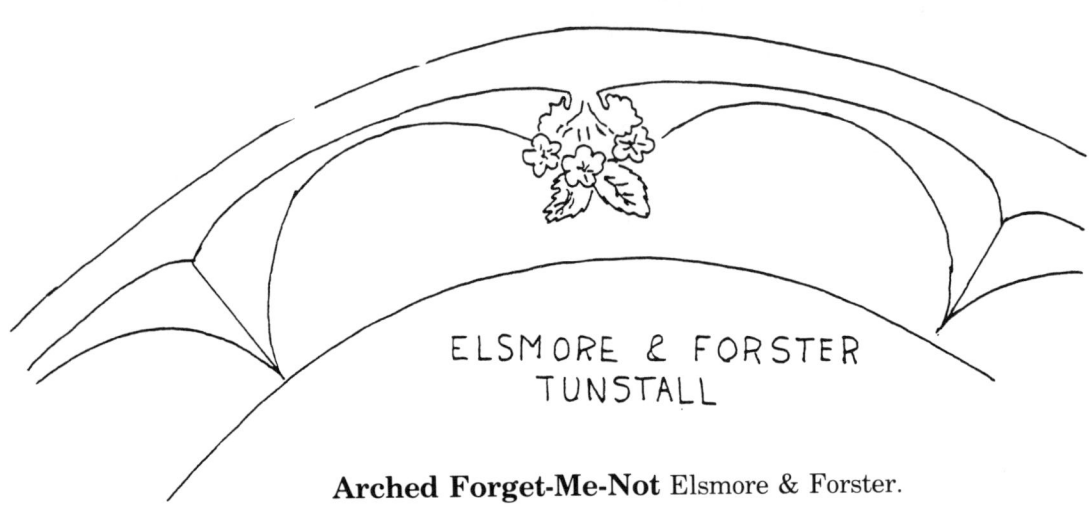

**Arched Forget-Me-Not** Elsmore & Forster.

**Garden Sprig** J. & G. Meakin. Five motifs around plates.

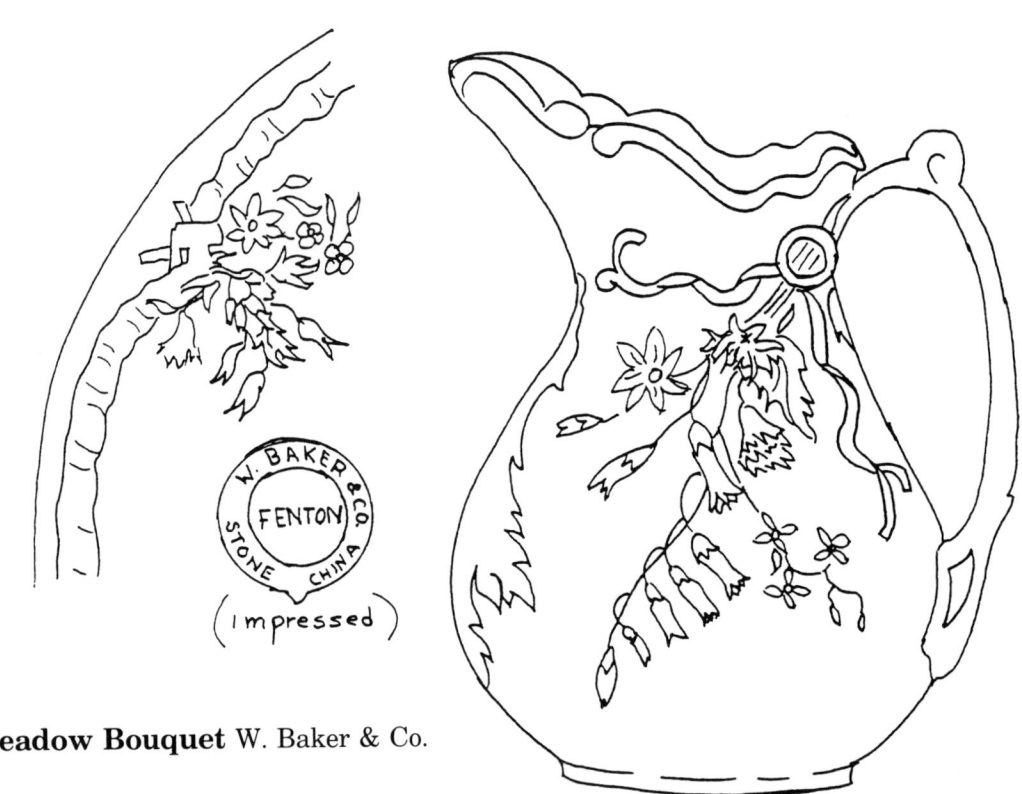

**Meadow Bouquet** W. Baker & Co.

**Moss Rose** J. & G. Meakin. Motif detail on end of liner for soup tureen. Serving pieces are bulbous in shape. The teapot handle is forked at the top.

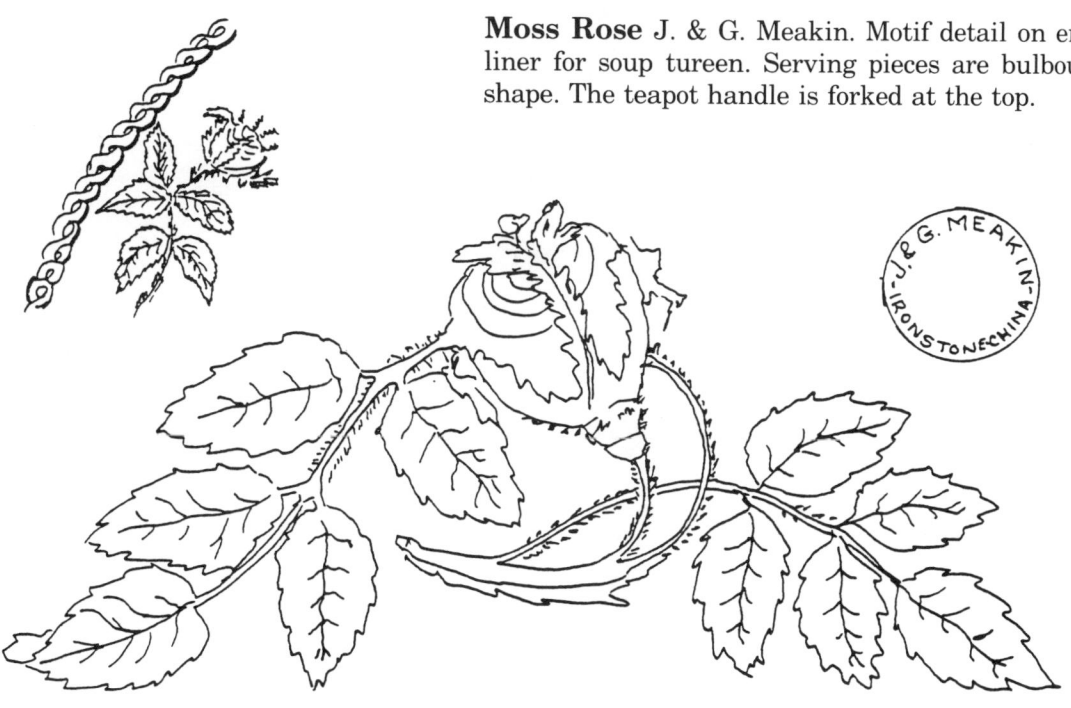

**Fuchsia** George Jones and J. & G. Meakin.

60. *FUCHSIA vegetable server by J. & G. Meakin. Photograph: Blair.*

**Laurel** Wedgwood & Co.

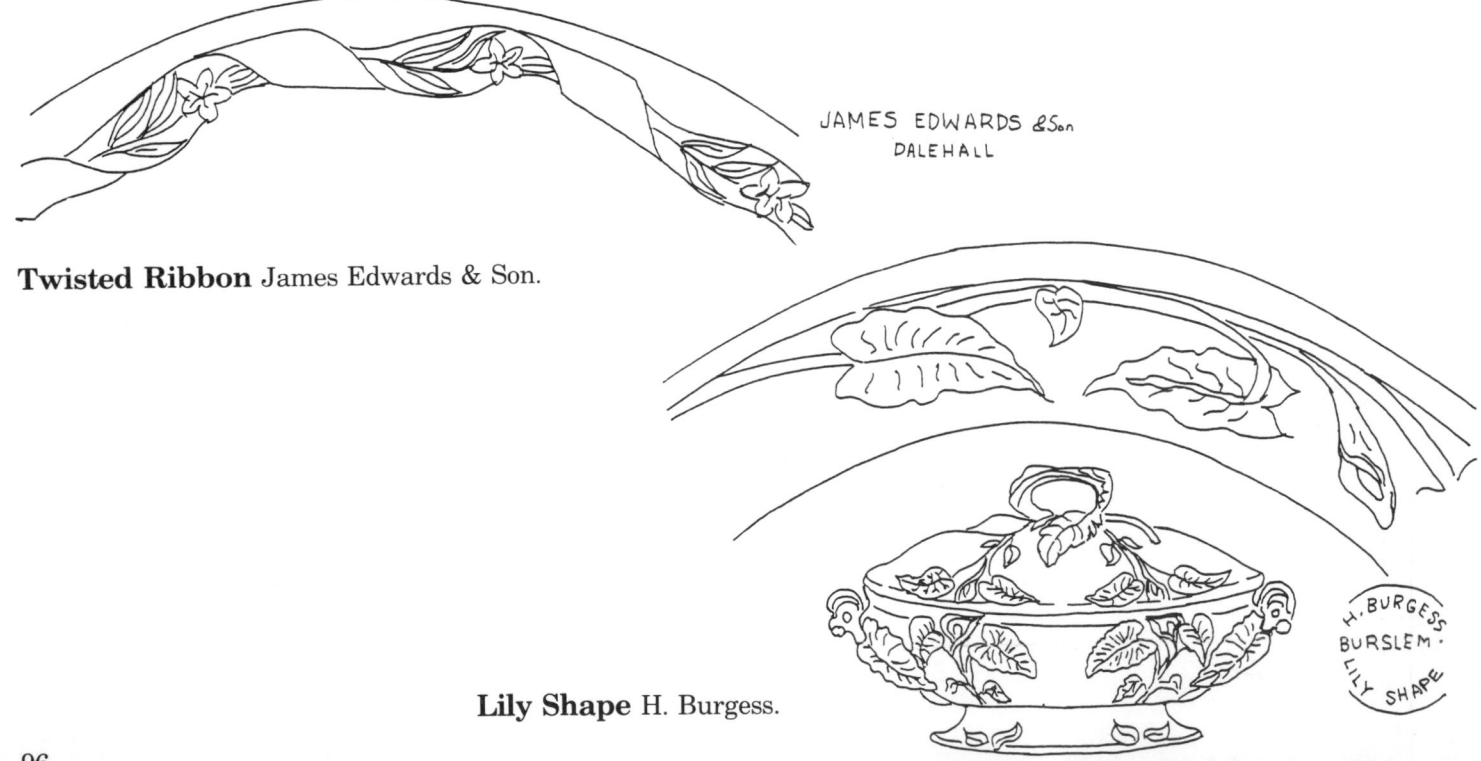

61. LAUREL *teapot liberally decorated by Wedgwood & Co.* FUCHSIA *handleless cup and saucer. Collection of Mr. and Mrs. John Black, New York. Photograph: Black.*

**Nosegay** E. & C. Challinor. This dainty design is repeated five times.

**Twisted Ribbon** James Edwards & Son.

**Lily Shape** H. Burgess.

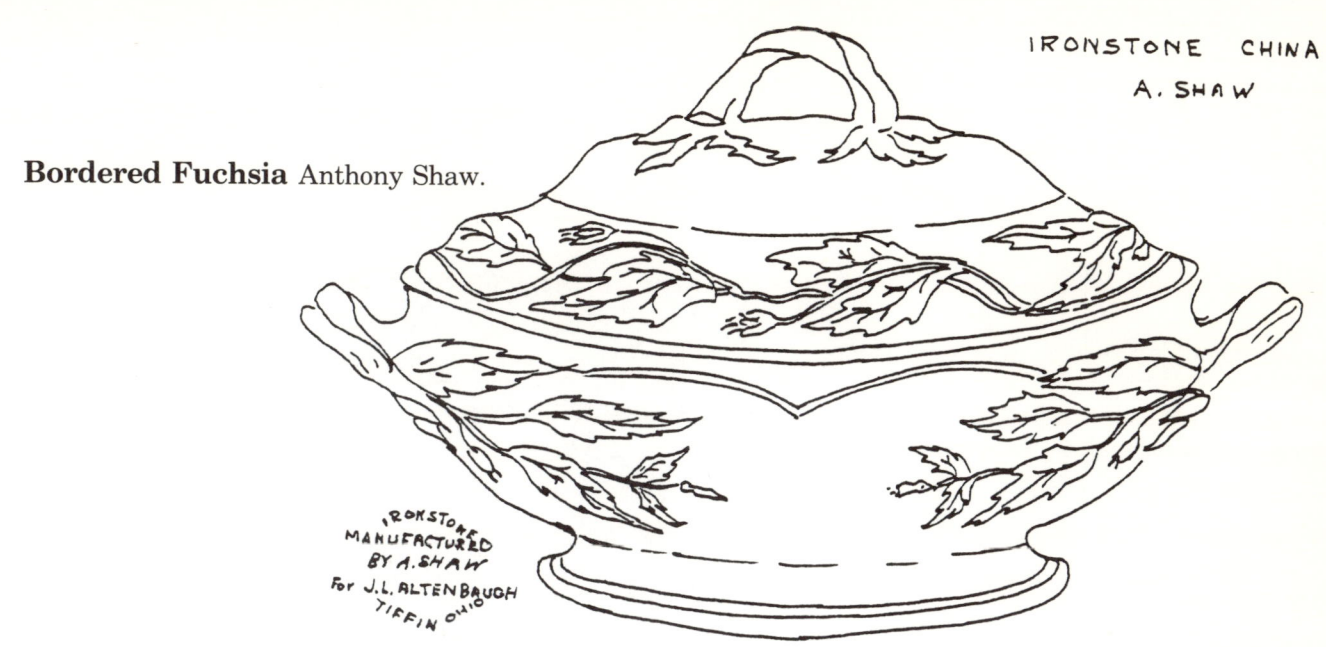

IRONSTONE CHINA
A. SHAW

**Bordered Fuchsia** Anthony Shaw.

**Trumpet Vine** Liddle, Elliott & Son. Most pieces include the 1865 registry date but omit the potter's name.

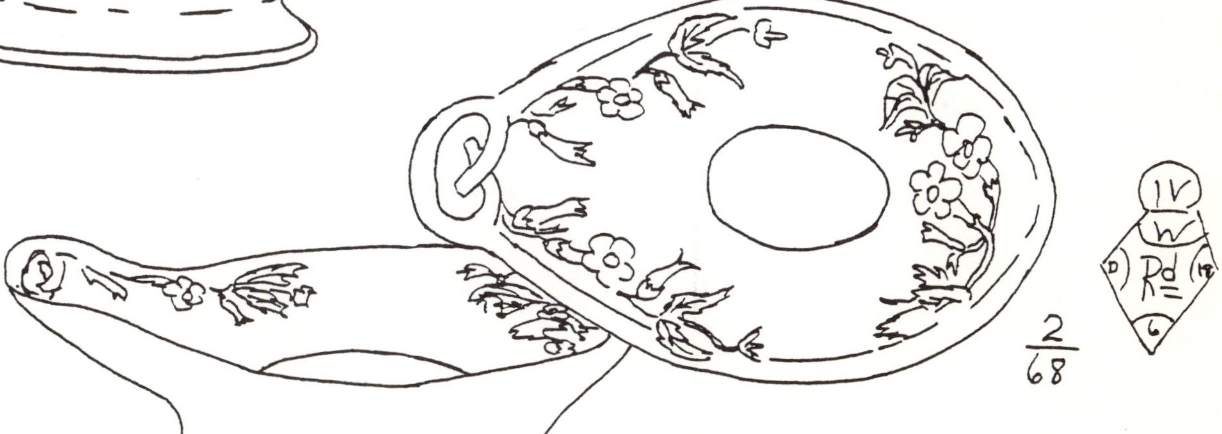

**Wild Rose Twig** C. Meigh & Son after 1860.

**Bellflower** James Edwards.

62. BELLFLOWER *waste bowl from a tea set and teapot by J. Edwards. Collection of James and Doris Walker, New York. Photograph: Blair.*

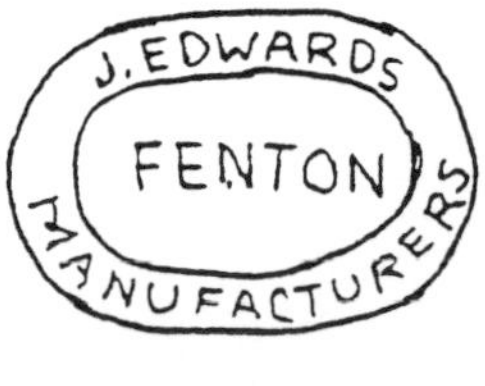

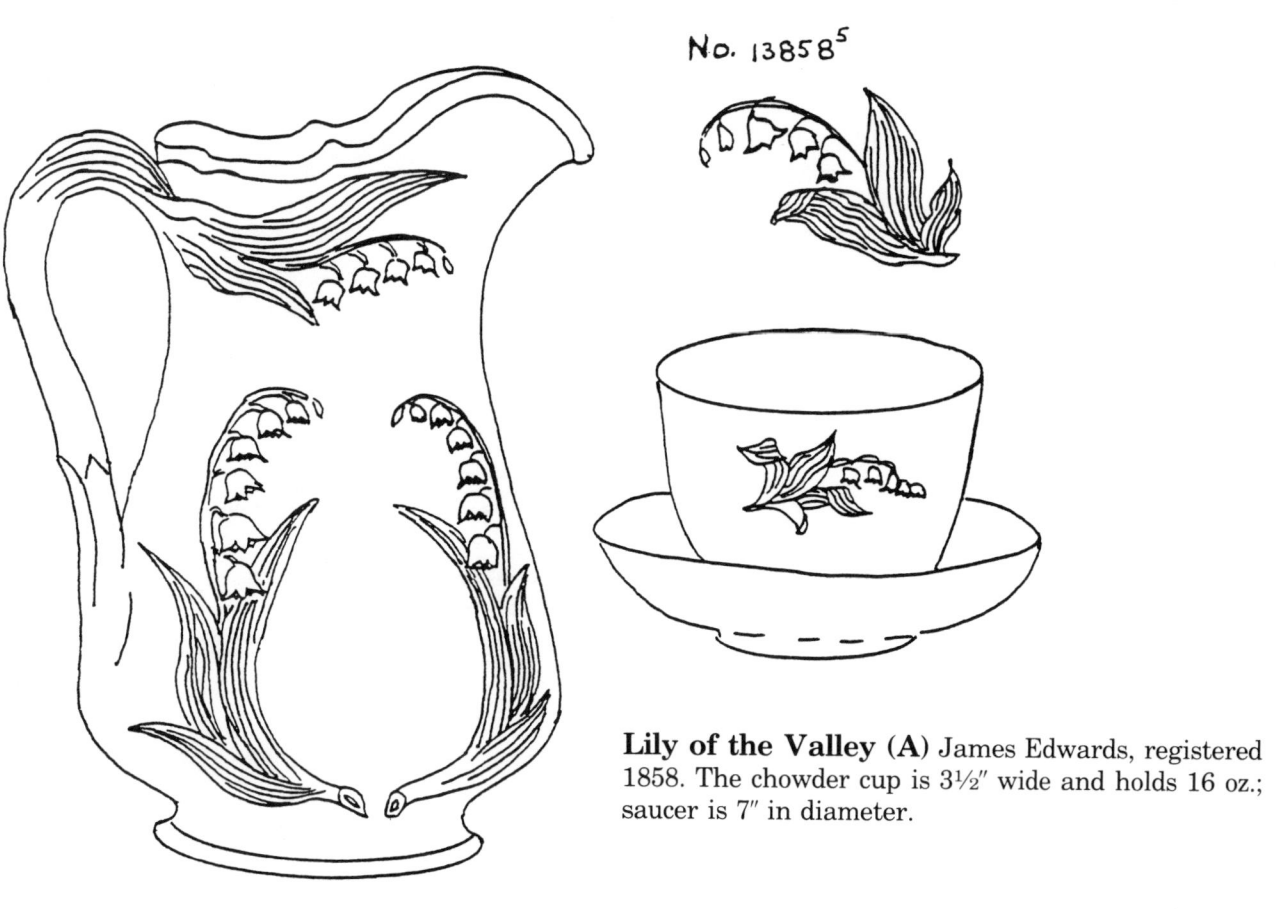

**Lily of the Valley (A)** James Edwards, registered 1858. The chowder cup is 3½″ wide and holds 16 oz.; saucer is 7″ in diameter.

**Hyacinth** Wedgwood & Co.

**Bordered Hyacinth** W. Baker & Co.

**Western Shape** Hope & Carter, W. & E. Corn, registered 1862.

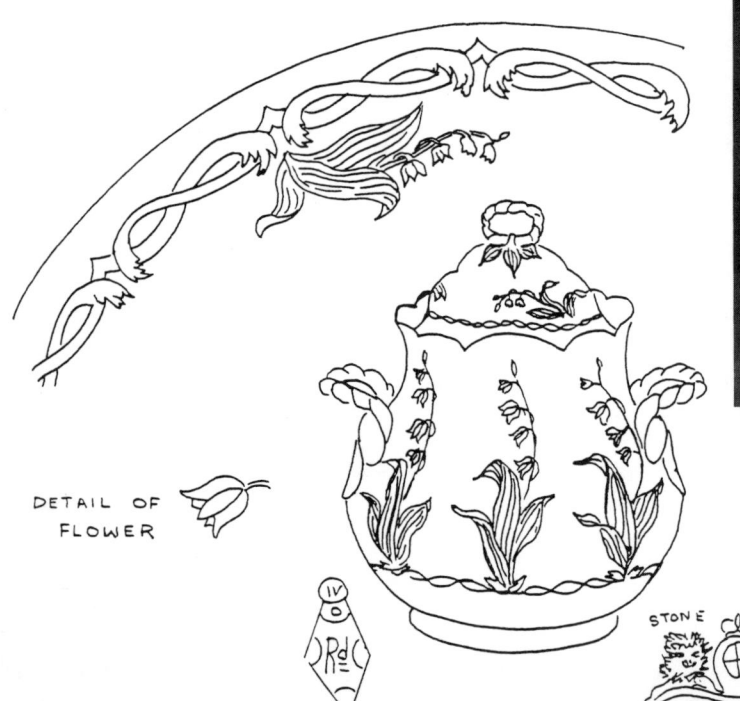

63. Lily of the Valley motif is shown on WESTERN SHAPE sugar bowl by W. & E. Corn and toddy cup by Anthony Shaw. Collection of James and Doris Walker. Photograph: Blair.

**Shaw's Lily of the Valley** Anthony Shaw. Finial is a large, three-dimensional bellflower. This design has been found on bone dishes which were not usual pieces in a set of early white ironstone.

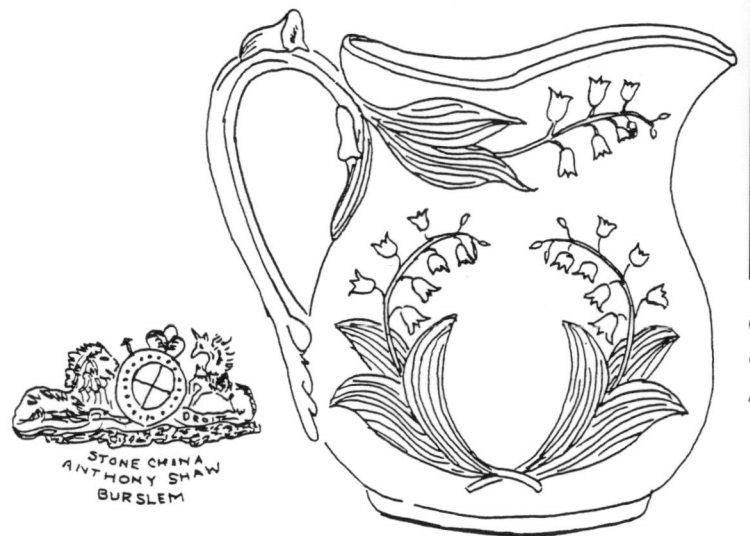

*64. SHAW'S LILY OF THE VALLEY bellflower finial and small bellflowers on sides of stalk. Collection of Winfield and Lyn Wetherbee. Photograph: Blair.*

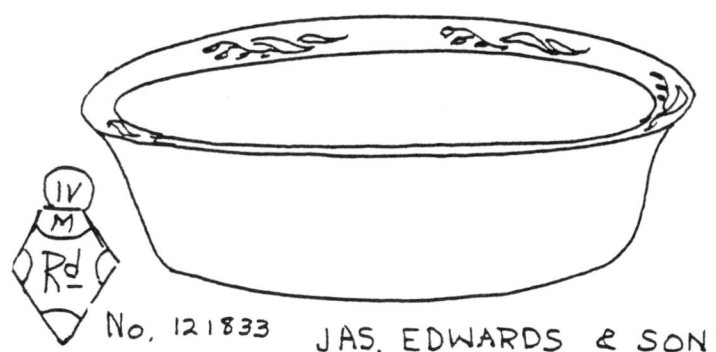

**Lily of the Valley (B)** James Edwards & Son. This small, oval server reveals that the Edwards firm revived an old pattern, LILY OF THE VALLEY (A), with vague impressed lines.

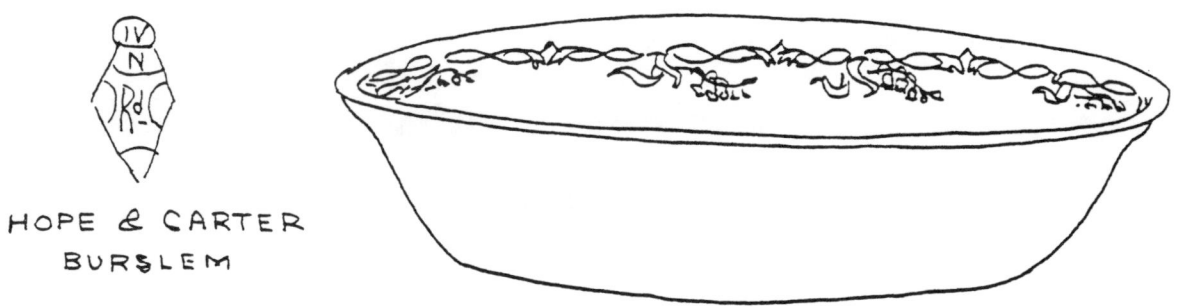

**Little Western** Hope & Carter. Here we discover that this firm produced WESTERN SHAPE in miniature in 1864, two years after the original design was introduced.

101

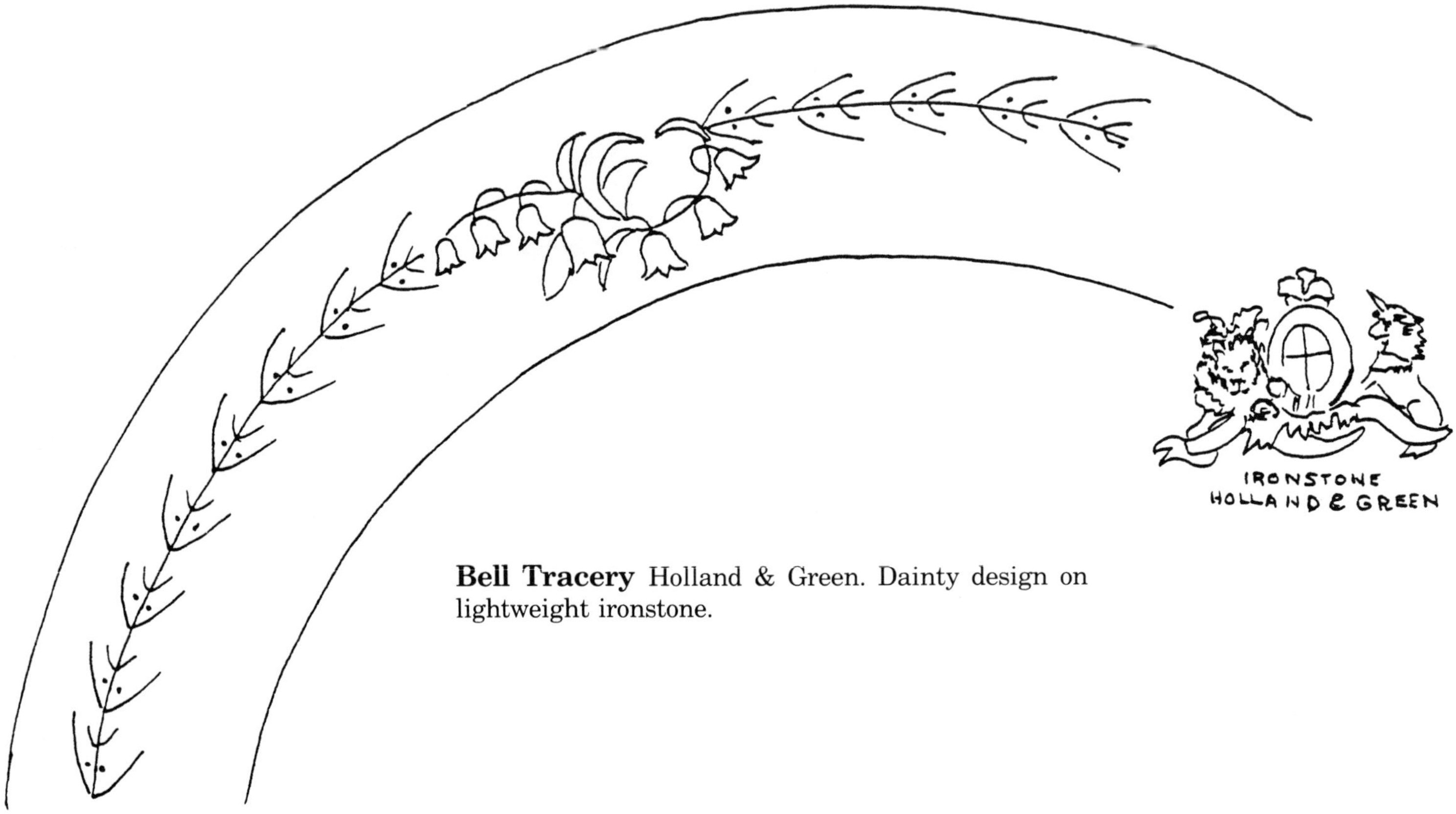

**Bell Tracery** Holland & Green. Dainty design on lightweight ironstone.

**Fruit Garden** Potted by J. F. These plates were completely covered by fruit, foliage, and blooms. Even the background was stippled.

# XIII  Ribs and Revival

Two other types of motifs were repeated often enough to warrant our discussion. These were narrow ribbing and a minor revival of old Grecian patterns and names.

In the 1860s, some of the Staffordshire potters covered the borders of plates and the bodies of serving dishes with ribs. Meakin's *Ribbed Raspberry with Bloom* and Pankhurst's *Ribbed Chain* made very similar tureens covered with narrow ribs, borders, and foliage and equipped them with twig finials and handles. J.W. Pankhurst used the ribbed decoration more often than other manufacturers.

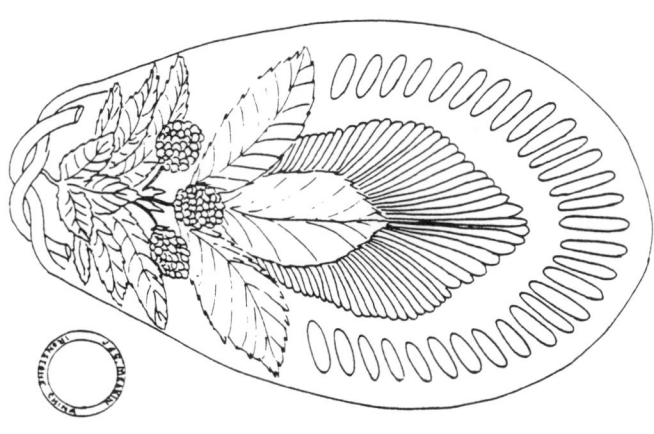

**Ribbed Raspberry with Bloom** J. & G. Meakin. The bodies of all servers were covered with design. Tureens included the blossoms as well as the berries, leaves, ribs, and grooves.

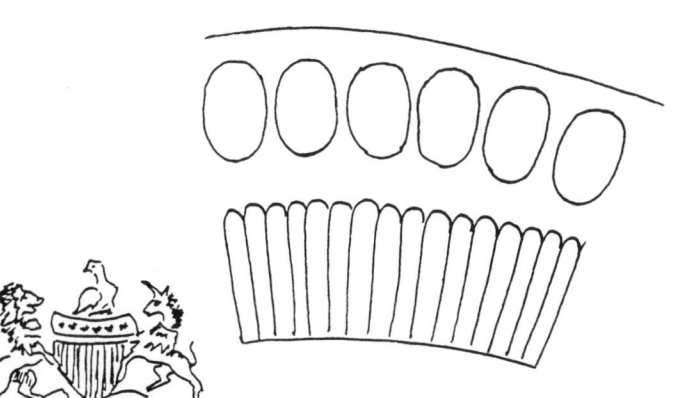

*65. RIBBED RASPBERRY WITH BLOOM by J. & G. Meakin is a pattern that covers most of the bodies of serving dishes and the complete borders of plates. Blooms are seen on covers. Collection of John Black. Photograph: Black.*

**Ribbed Berry** John Alcock. Detail of leaves with berries molded over the narrow ribs of a pitcher.

67. *RIBBED BERRY pitcher by John Alcock showing decoration superimposed on ribs. Owned by James and Doris Walker, New York. Photograph: Blair.*

66. *RIBBED BUD sauce tureen by Pankhurst. Buds on the finial, under the handle, and on the ends of the tray are checked. Collection of John and Jane Yunginger, Minnesota. Photograph: Blair.*

**Ribbed Chain** J. W. Pankhurst. Covered serving dishes were fully decorated with chain, ribs, and foliage, and used twisted twig handles.

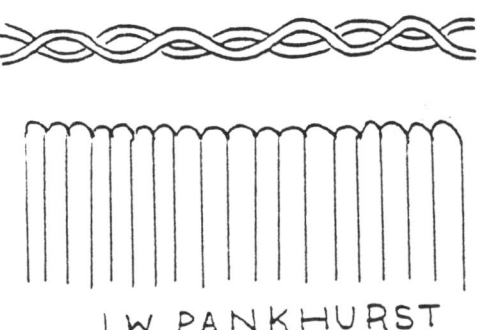

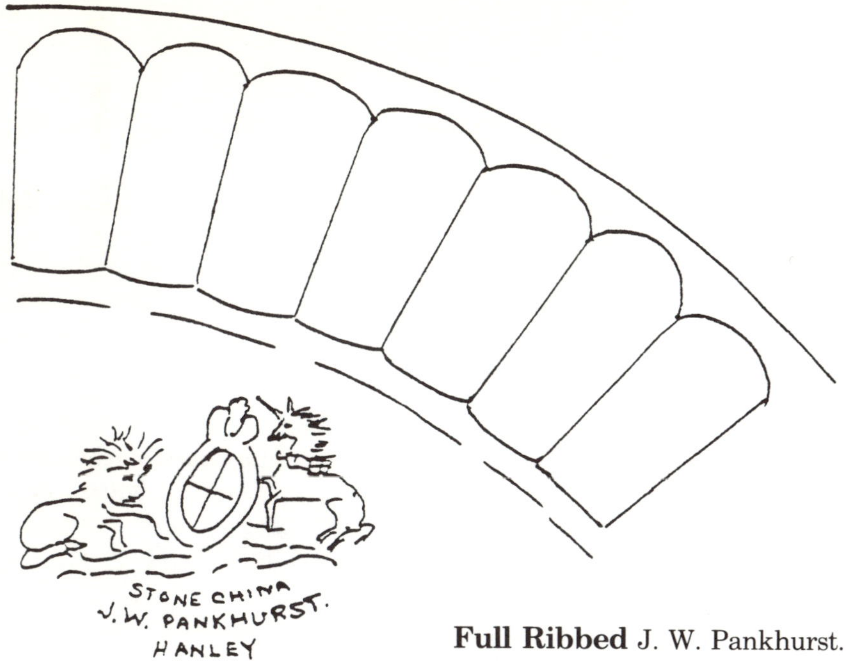

**Full Ribbed** J. W. Pankhurst.

**Dover Shape** W. Adams, registered 1862.

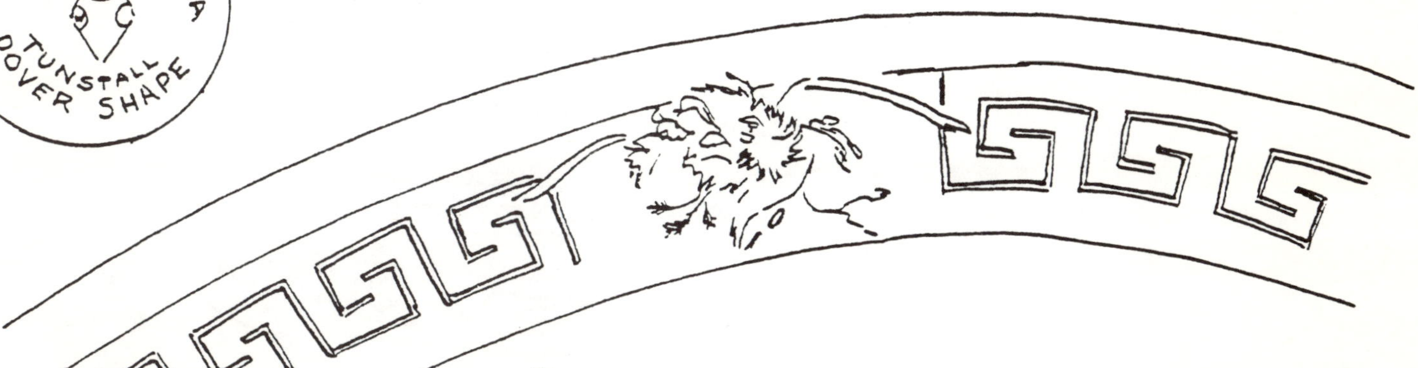

**Athena Shape** No potter's name on the three plates I have seen. The registry date is 1865.

105

A small classic revival was seen in clothes and furniture during the later half of the nineteenth century. In the late 1860s this influence reached the china businesses. Therefore, we find Greek and Roman Key borders, the fleur-de-lis, Wall of Troy and other geometric bands, victory wreaths, and laurel leaves decorating some of the dishes shaped at that time. *ATHENA SHAPE, ATHENIA,* and *ATHENS SHAPE* are naturally often confused because of the similar names.

Collectors have often believed Jones' *Victor Shape* to be the same as Elsmore & Forster's *Laurel Wreath*. A close study of the photographs and drawings that follow will reveal the differences: *Victor* has corn in its wreath while *Laurel Wreath* has a star at the top of its ring of leaves. I hope you can find some pieces to compare. Both patterns are hoarded by collectors.

Although two other revival patterns (*Olympic Shape* by Elsmore & Forster, registered in 1864, and *Wall of Troy* produced by J. W. Pankhurst in 1863) are not depicted, both have been described by Pauline Meissen-Helter in her unpublished work, *What Is Ironstone*. Of *Olympic Shape* she stated, "The round bulbous coffee pot has a wide embossed Roman Key band circling the body near the base, above and adjacent to the band is a narrow border of beaded scroll work. A double band of the same work circles the neck. The straight handle and spout are finely ribbed."

Pankhurst's *Wall of Troy* was described as follows: "A wide Wall of Troy band circles the round body near the base; from the top of the handle and spreading across both sides of the body are branches of oak leaves; the lid has an acorn finial resting on oak leaves."

These patterns were used in the United States after the close of the Civil War by those families who could still afford to refurbish their tables.

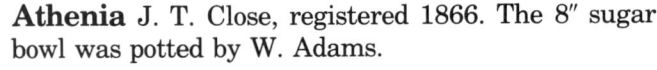

**Athenia** J. T. Close, registered 1866. The 8" sugar bowl was potted by W. Adams.

**Athens Shape** Podmore Walker & Co., registry date blurred. Nicknamed FLEUR DE LIS, this pattern was also sometimes marked Wedgwood & Co., the name of the above firm after 1860.

**Greek Key** J. W. Pankhurst.

**Victor Shape** registered 1868 by F. Jones & Co. Detail of wreath and plate border of corn with foliage.

68. VICTOR SHAPE pitcher potted by F. Jones. Owned by John and Jane Yunginger, Minnesota. Photograph: Blair.

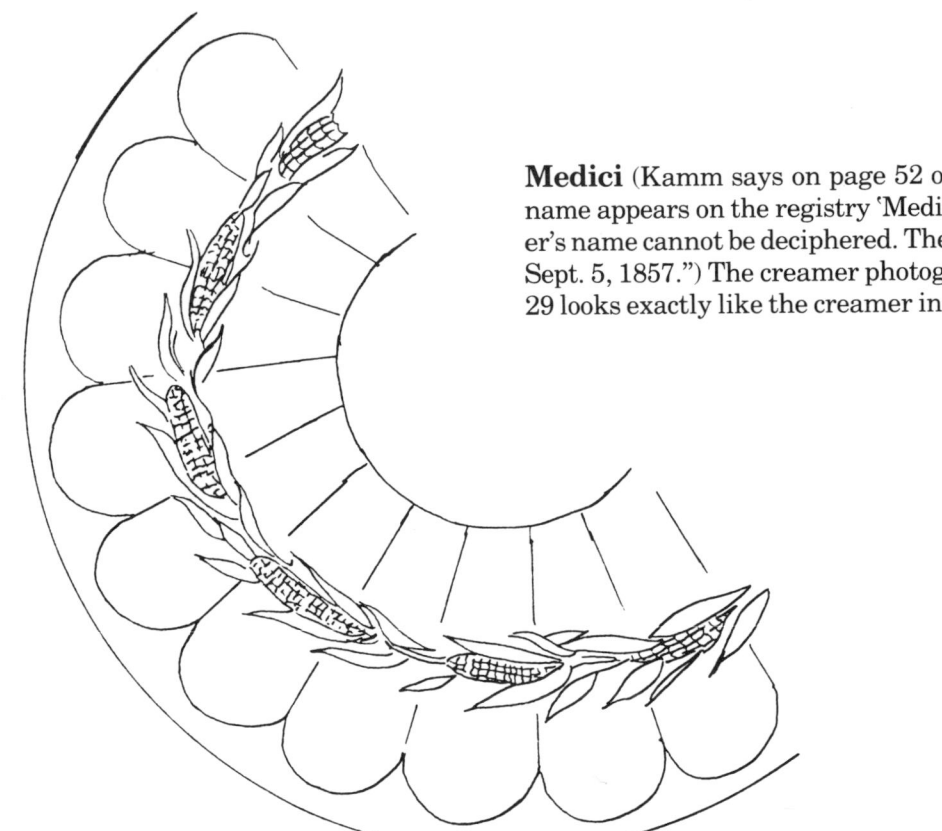

**Medici** (Kamm says on page 52 of her *Old China* "A name appears on the registry 'Medici' . . . manufacturer's name cannot be deciphered. The date can be read as Sept. 5, 1857.") The creamer photographed in her Plate 29 looks exactly like the creamer in our Photograph 68.

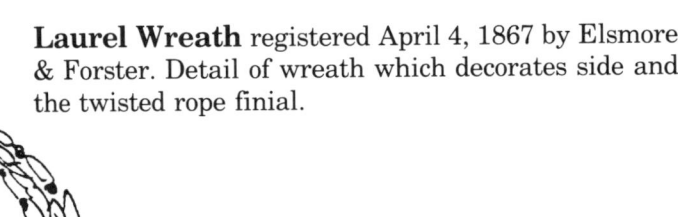

**Laurel Wreath** registered April 4, 1867 by Elsmore & Forster. Detail of wreath which decorates side and the twisted rope finial.

69. LAUREL WREATH *pieces potted by Elsmore & Forster. Owned by Mrs. Jane Diemer, Delaware. Photograph: Diemer.*

# XIV  Patterns of the Seventies and Eighties

After the decade of the sixties when realistic flowers and leaves profusely covered white ironstone, two new shapes were repeatedly seen. The first was found in graceful, plain lines on round bodies; the second employed square and rectangular lines. White ironstone (white graniteware) made by American potters echoed these contours.

The *Eagle, Lion's Head,* the two *Grape Cluster* designs, and *Budded Vine* possessed pitchers and teapots with pear-shaped bodies. In the following years, homemakers were to buy inexpensive sets with similar plain flowing lines.

About the same time, rectangular shapes became popular. Square butter pats and little square saucedishes were parts of many of these sets. The handled cups had straight slanting sides while the cup saucers were flat with slanting outer walls. Vegetable dishes were potted with and without covers. The covered butter dish was used during those years and is not to be confused with the covered soap dishes made ten or twenty years earlier.

By the seventies and eighties the great soup and chowder tureens no longer reigned at the head and foot of the large family tables. About then too, the covered sauce tureen yielded place to the open gravy boat. Before this, both were used together.

Lighter, creamier ironstone dinnerware and toilet sets were decorated in one-color brown or black with leaves, birds, or occasionally animals with an added scene in a small round or square frame. Often a diagonal geometric band slanted across part of the design. Most of these sets had the pattern name printed on the underside next to the late diamond-shaped registry mark or the registry number. This field of ceramics is available for research because little has been recorded about these interesting sets.

Mention must be made of *Cable and Ring,* and *Plain Uplift,* since so many potters used these same designs. Each varied their pattern a little bit to justify their lack of originality.

By 1891, when the American law requiring imports to be marked with the country of origin became effective, most Staffordshire potters had forsaken the production of cheap white ironstone except for hotel ware. They were already busily engaged in perfecting finer china bodies to tempt the American housewife.

*70. EAGLE, DOVE, or DIAMOND AND THUMBPRINT are nicknames of this unique shape. These pieces potted by Gelson Brothers. Collection of Gary and Carol Grove, Pennsylvania.*

**Eagle** Gelson Bros. registered in 1869 may have been designed with the 1876 Centennial in mind. This pattern has also been called DOVE or DIAMOND AND THUMBPRINT.

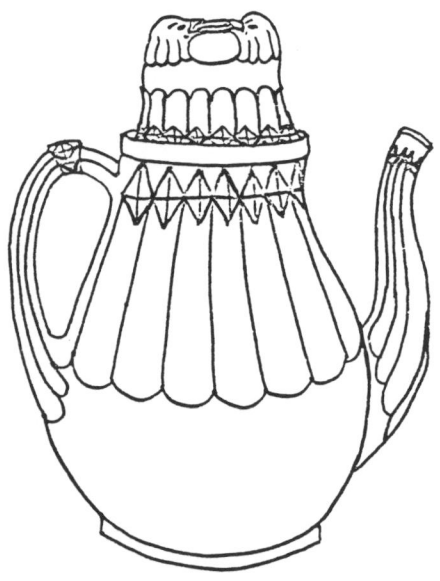 

*71. JUMBO pitcher, named for the elephant head on the handle. Owned by Mr. and Mrs. John Black. Photograph: Black.*

**Seashore Shape** W. E. Corn, after 1868 registry descernible on all pieces I have seen, but in each the letter designating the year is not clear.

72. SEASHORE toilet set pieces owned by the Hoggs of Canajoharie, New York, potted by W. & E. Corn. The lines of the toothbrush holder, soap dish, and pitcher are generally rectangular. From an exhibit at the Fort Plain Museum, Fort Plain, New York. Photograph: Blair.

**Grape Clusters** Davenport.

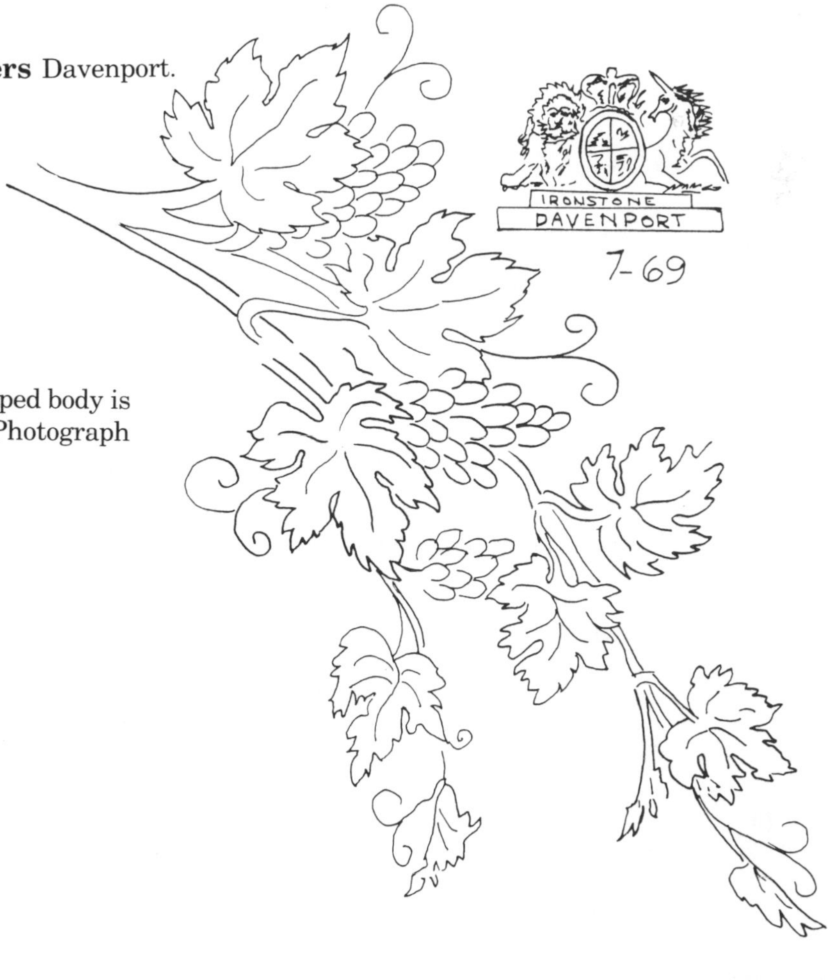

**Jumbo** Henry Alcock. The plain, pear-shaped body is characteristic of most 1880s patterns. (See Photograph 71.)

**Grape Cluster with Chain** Henry Burgess. Motif taken from the side of a large milk jug.

73. GRAPE CLUSTERS *chamber pot made by Davenport in 1869 and* GRAPE CLUSTER WITH CHAIN *large jug. Two closely related, vintage patterns. Photograph: Blair.*

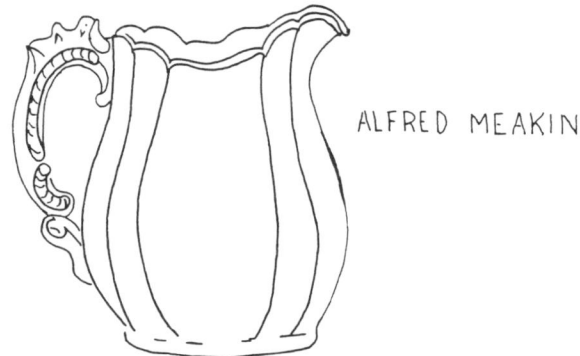

**Double Panel** Alfred Meakin.

**Budded Vine** Meakin & Co., some pieces marked Meakin Bros. This pattern reflects the body decorations of the 1860s on the body lines of the seventies and eighties.

74. BUDDED VINE *tureen by Meakin & Co., impressed potting date, 1888. Main lines of the body are very like the plain dishes potted in the 1880s. Collection of Jean Hogg, New York. Photograph: Blair.*

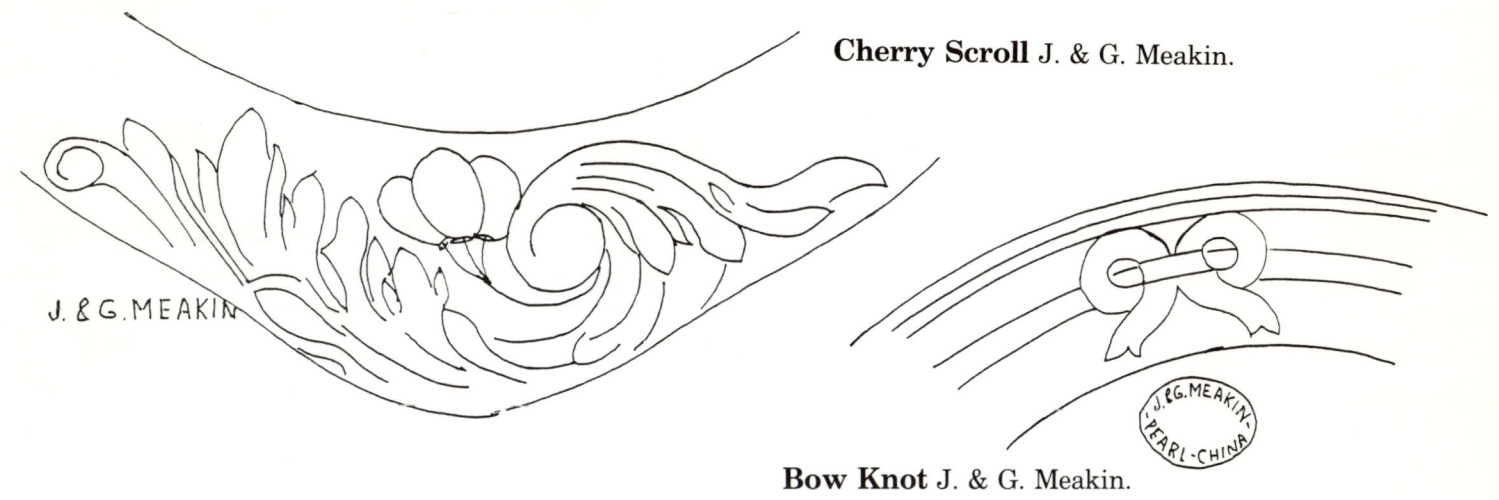

**Cherry Scroll** J. & G. Meakin.

**Bow Knot** J. & G. Meakin.

**Little Palm** T. & R. Boote, late greyhound stamp, circa 1880.

**Lion's Head** (or Sheep's Head as named by Kamm) John Edwards, late diamond-shaped registry illegible. Other collectors have tagged this design *Ram's Head* but the animal head looks to me like it was taken right off the king of the jungle.

**Square Ridged** Wedgwood & Co.

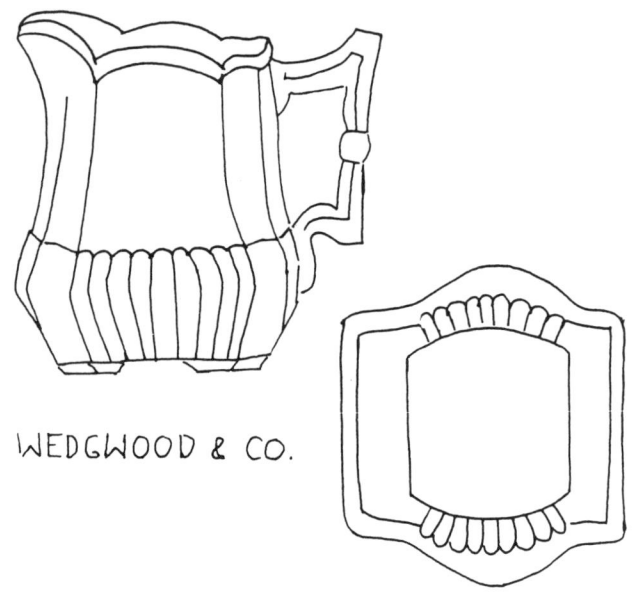

75. SQUARE RIDGED *collection of Johnson Bros. ironstone made during the last decades of the nineteenth century. Owned by Mr. and Mrs. John Black, New York. Photograph: Black.*

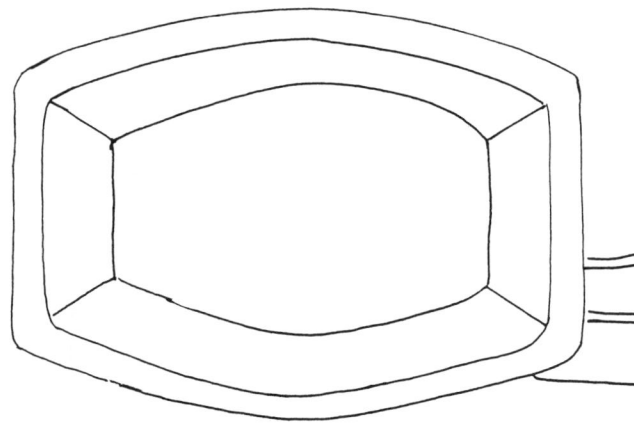

**Curved Rectangle** Charles Meakin.

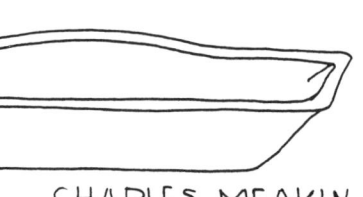

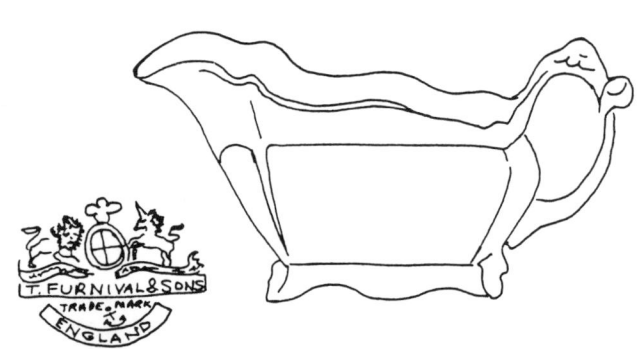

**Gentle Square** Thomas Furnival & Sons, circa 1876.

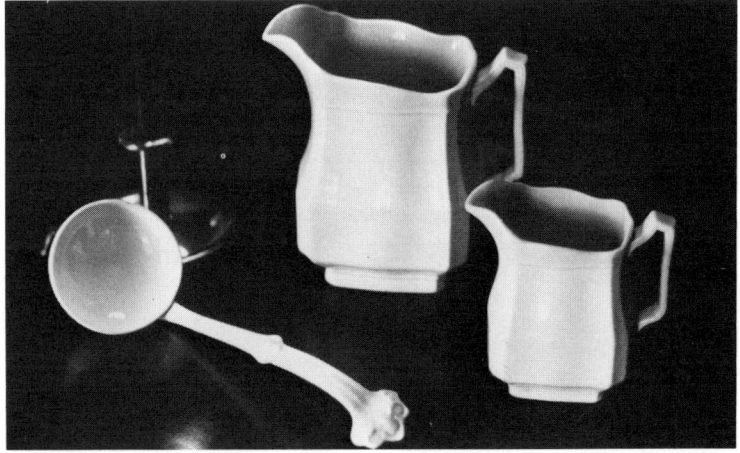

76. BLOCK OPTIC *or* MITERED BLOCK *pitchers by J. & G. Meakin. Collection of Mr. and Mrs. William Horner, Delaware. Photograph: Dr. Horner.*

**Cable and Ring** J. & G. Meakin, John Maddock and Sons, Cockson & Chetwynd, Anthony Shaw, E. & C. Challinor, T. Furnival & Sons, William Adams and others from about 1875 to 1890. This popular design was also used by American potters.

# Plain Bodies
# Handle Details

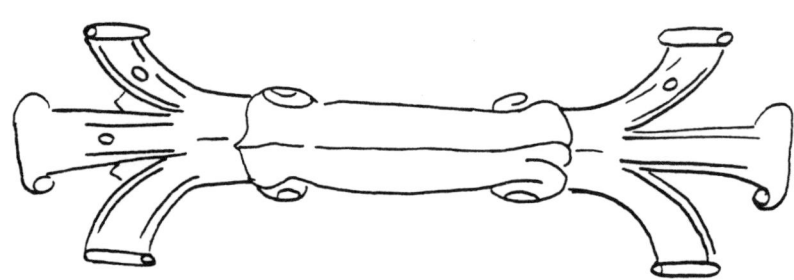

**Simplicity** John Maddock & Co.

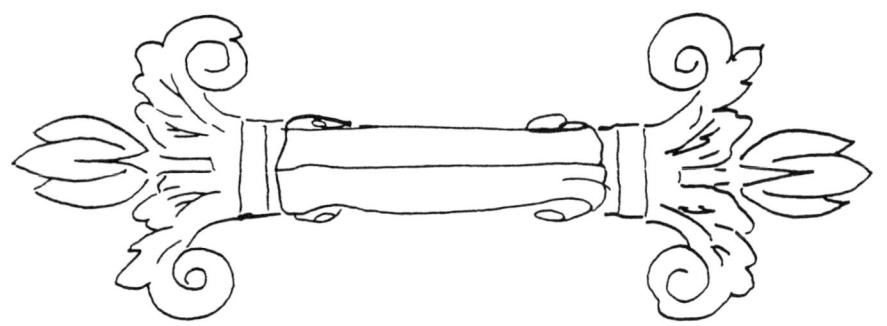

**Tulip** Wedgwood & Co.

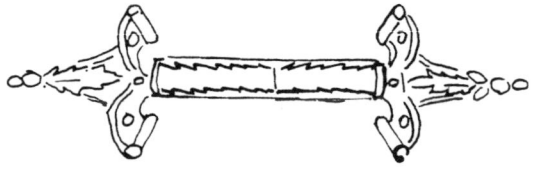

**Seine** John Edwards.

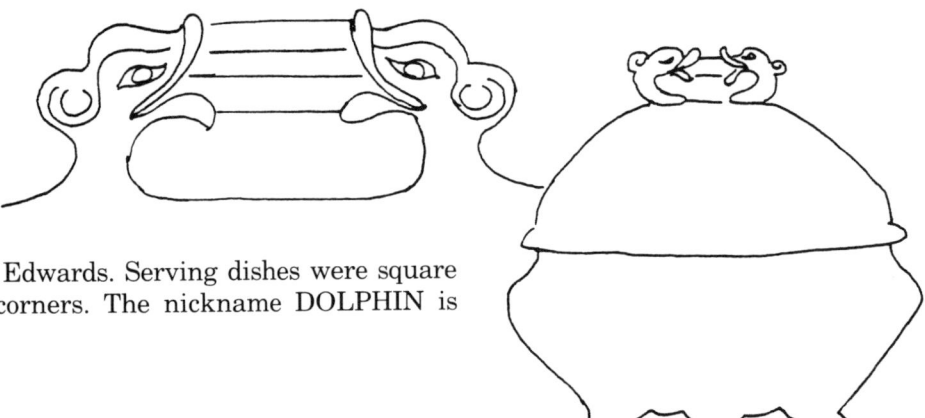

**Victory** John Edwards. Serving dishes were square with rounded corners. The nickname DOLPHIN is often used.

77. Maddock's SIMPLICITY is a good example of simple designs of the seventies and eighties. Most covered vegetables were oval and most soap dishes were round. SIMPLICITY was made in both shapes but the server shown is round and the soap dish is oval. From the collection of Stephen and Silvia Wetherbee, New York. Photograph: Blair.

**Senate** T. & R. Boote, registered 1870.

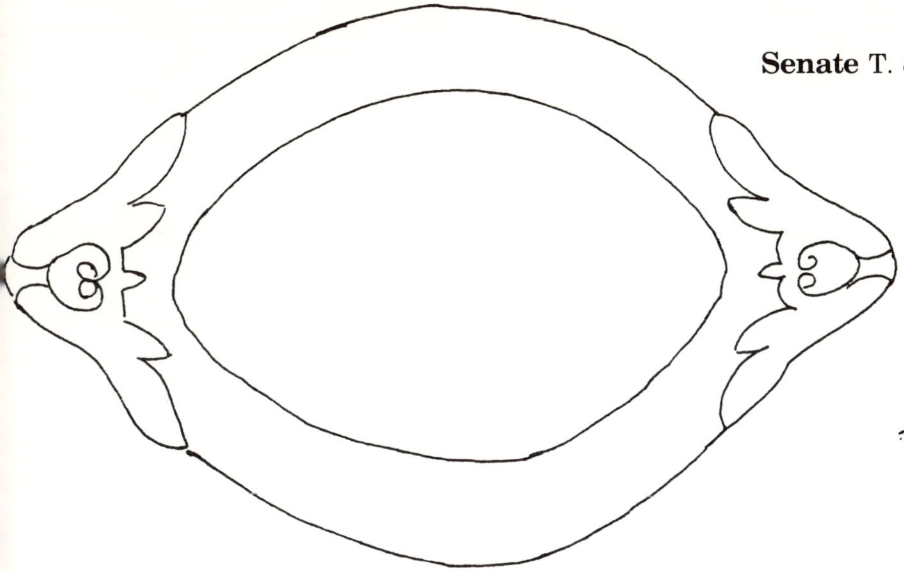

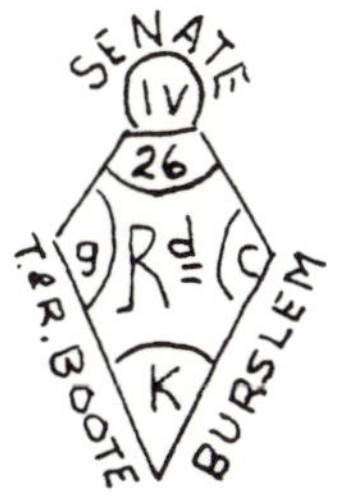

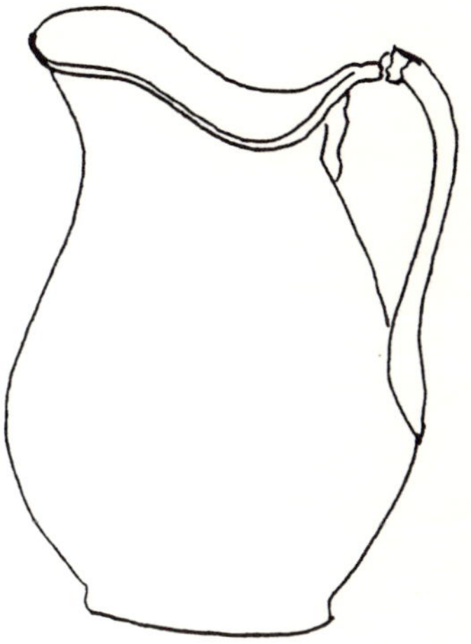

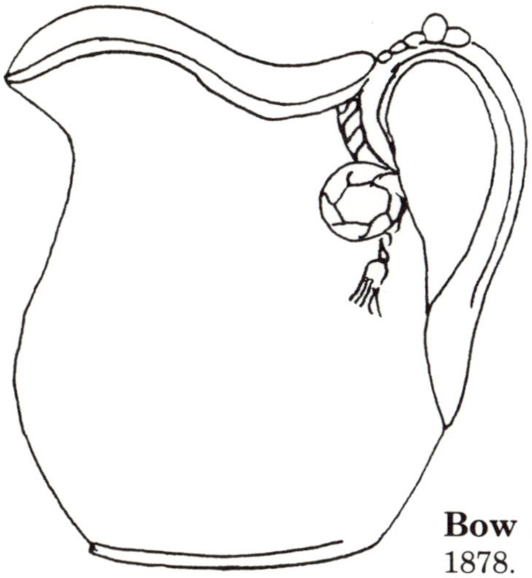

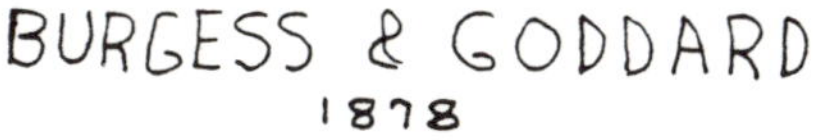

**Bow and Tassel** Burgess & Goddard, registered 1878.

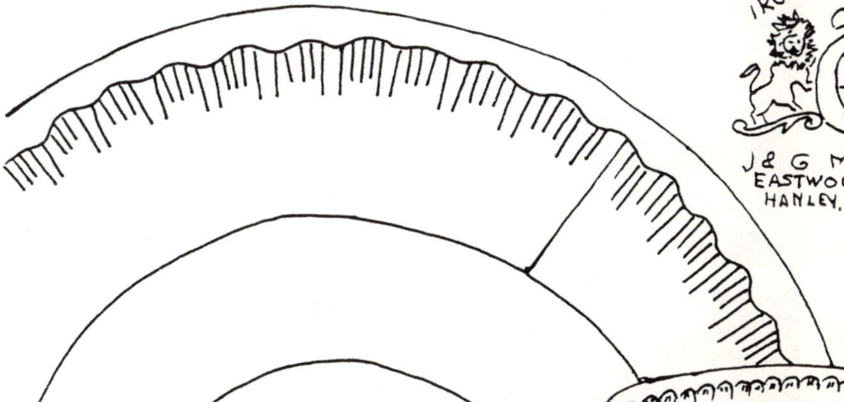

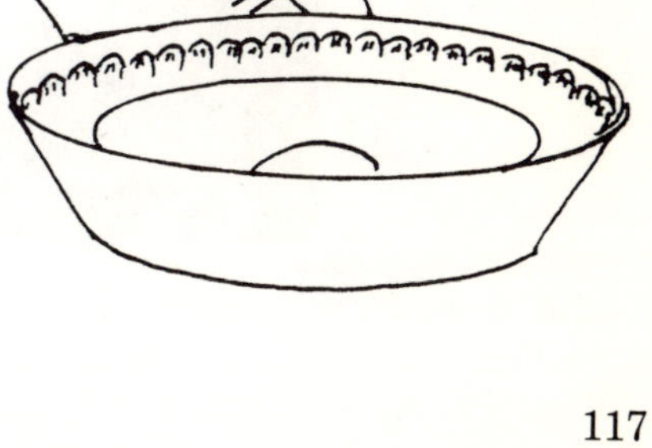

**Piecrust** J. & G. Meakin.

117

**Plain Uplift** Maddock & Gater, Clementson Bros., and many others. (See Photograph 78.)

**Plain** J. & G. Meakin, Burgess & Goddard, and most Staffordshire potters of the seventies and eighties.

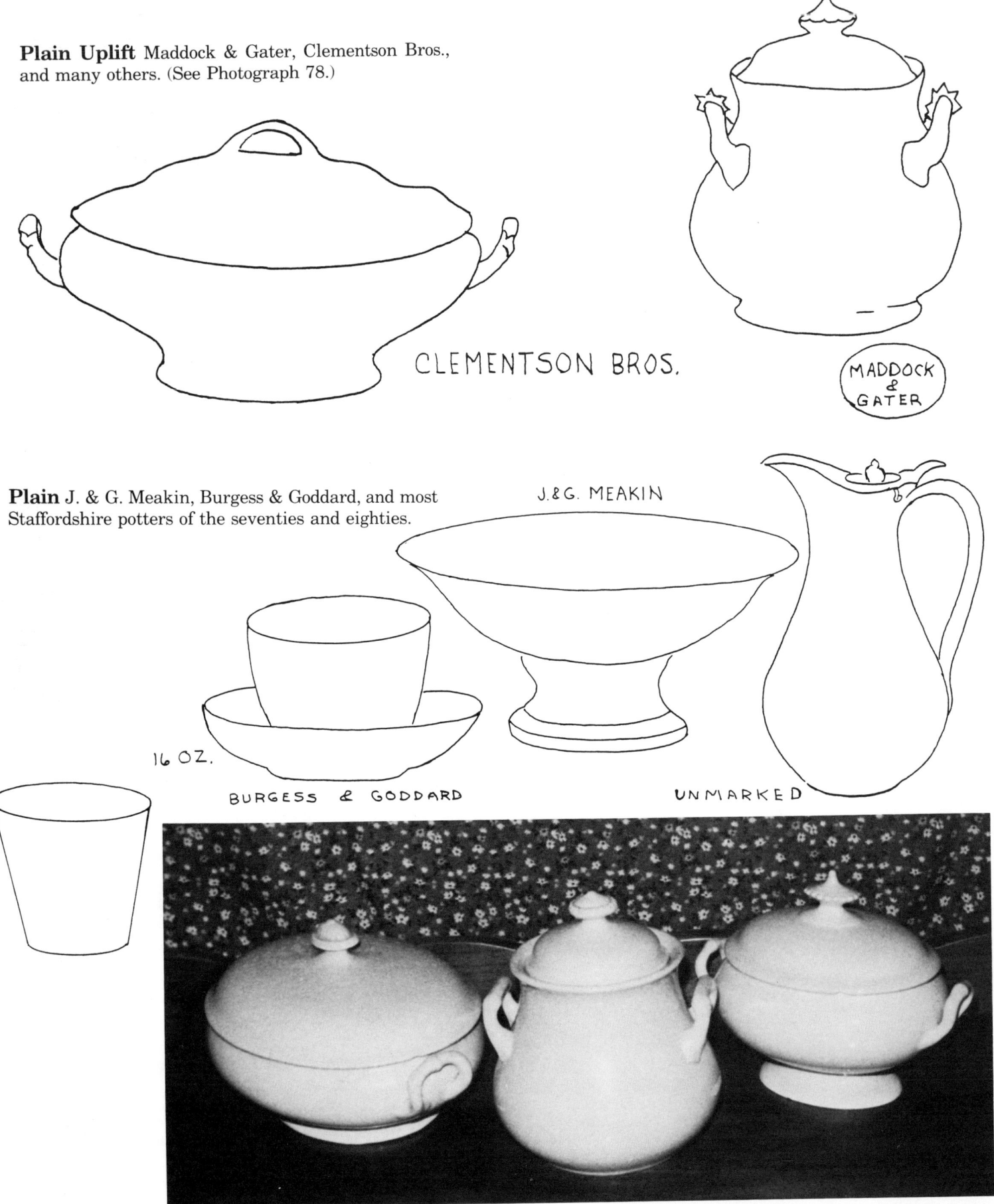

78. *PLAIN UPLIFT pieces, exemplifying lines of the 1870s and 1880s. Bodies are heavy at bottom, with handles which seem to lift upward; tops have acorn finials. Each piece was made by a different potter.*

79. Shallow finger dips, a Victorian novelty, potted by John Edwards after 1891. Owned by Mr. and Mrs. John Black. Photograph: Black.

81. SQUARE MELON-RIBBED nest of servers with scalloped edges over melon-shaped ribs by J. & G. Meakin. Other companies, both English and American, made similar sets offering even more sizes. Collection of Mr. and Mrs. John Black. Photograph: Black.

80. Syllabub bowl by T. & R. Boote, 10" diameter, 3½ quart size, with the words, "Royal Patent," included in the mark. Unmarked ladle, SCALLOPED DECAGON syllabub cup. Collection of Mr. and Mrs. John Black. Photograph: Black.

82. DRAPED LEAF (B) by James Edwards next to late, miniature, unmarked tea set. Cups to this set were unmarked

83. Long, slender platters for serving baked fish shown with bone dishes by J. & G. Meakin. Collection of Mr. and Mrs. John Black. Photograph: Black.

# XV   After 1891

A few Staffordshire potters still offered an occasional set in lighter weight white ironstone after the 1891 law. These were quite busy patterns as revealed by the two examples here. Enough collectors have written me to reveal an interest in gathering pieces especially of *Basketweave with Band* and Johnson Brothers' *Tracery*. In general, however, the offerings after this date were toilet sets and hotel ware.

As the Victorian Age accelerated, the American woman avidly purchased the semiporcelain and porcelain, flowered and gilded, sent from England to the beauty-starved American housewife. By the turn of the century, the dream of owning the translucent china from Germany, Austria, or Bavaria touched most American homes. The general attitude was, "China to be good must be imported."

**Basketweave with Band** Alfred Meakin, after 1891.

**Basketweave** Anthony Shaw, circa 1880 — beverage servers were square-bodied.

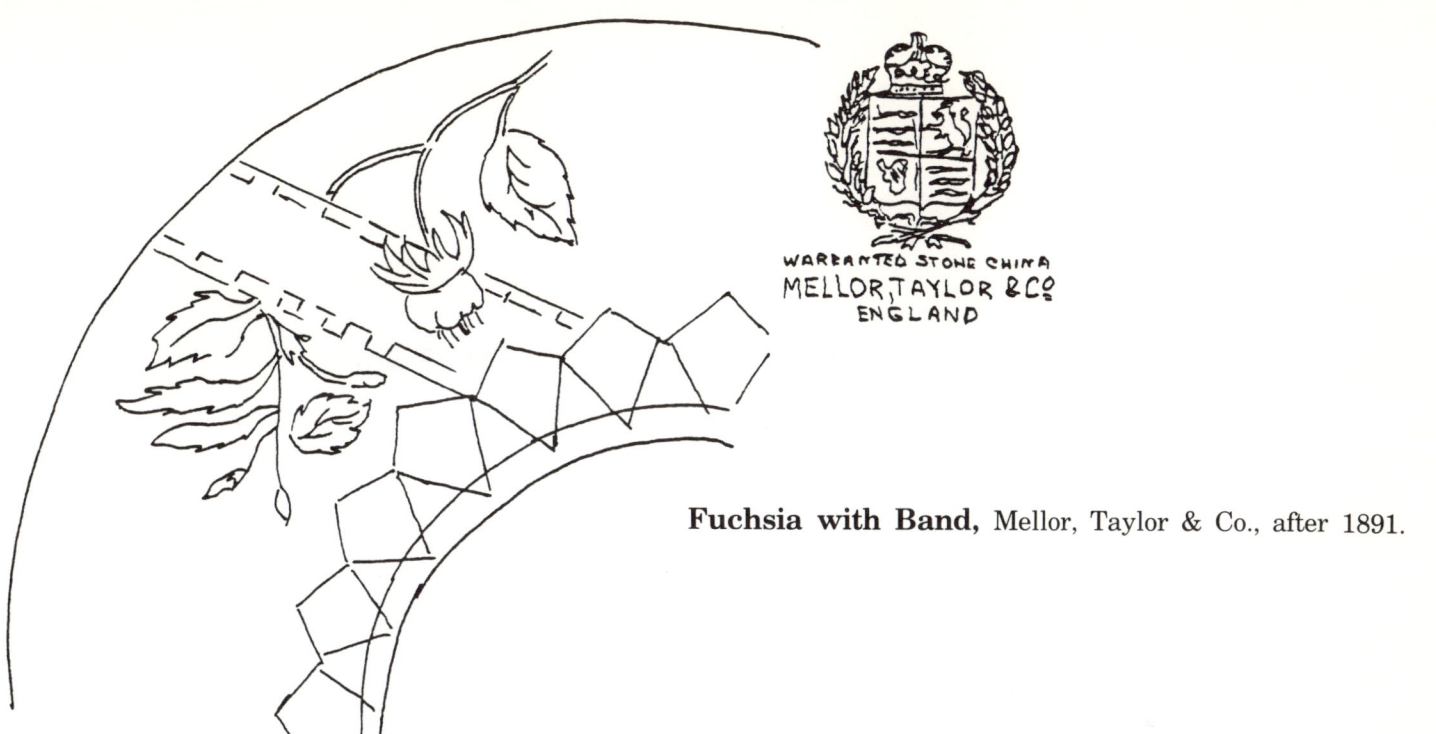

**Fuchsia with Band,** Mellor, Taylor & Co., after 1891.

**Tracery** Johnson Bros., after 1891.

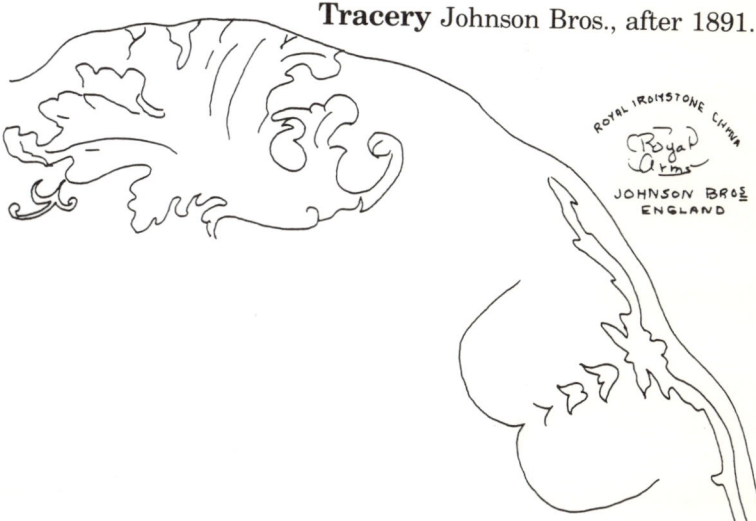

84. TRACERY, large, turn-of-the-century sugar bowl and creamer potted by Johnson Bros. Collection of Karl and Linda Dalenberg, Massachusetts.

**Flower Garden Border** W. H. Grindley & Co., after 1891.

# XVI  Copper Tea Leaf Ironstone

"How did you happen not to include information about *Copper Tea Leaf* in your handbook?"

"Where can I find out more about Copper Tea Leaf Ironstone?"

Such questions were asked me by readers of *White Ironstone*. I haven't really explored in that area but other collectors are gathering facts. Someday when you see a book published on this subject, you'll exclaim, "Just what I've been waiting for!" Meanwhile, here's just a little information.

Collectors of this pattern generally agree to give Anthony Shaw credit for the first use of the well-known three copper lustre leaves decorating white ironstone. The original name of this design was *Lustre Band and Sprig* or *Lustre Spray*. Twentieth century collectors must have christened this pattern *Copper Tea Leaf* since old advertisements never used these words.

Today, we run across some dishes that reveal that experimentation preceded the wide use of this pattern in the 1880s. Elsmore & Forster took their popular 1859 *Ceres Shape* and covered the wheat heads and stalks with color: soft glowing chocolate or two shades of bright blue or golden grain with green shards. None of these sets was as attractive or as popular as the original all-white *Ceres*. This firm tried adding color to some other shapes such as two shades of blue on *Little Scroll*, shown on the sugar bowl in Photograph 88.

85. PORTLAND SHAPE by Elsmore & Forster with added copper tea leaf lustre decor. Owned by Mr. and Mrs. William Horner. Photograph: Horner.

On the 1858 *New York Shape,* Joseph Clementson added a motif with a finished appearance very like the later *Lustre Band and Sprig*. An application of greenish brown was introduced under the glaze in bands around the edges and on a center motif more detailed than the final tea leaf design. After glazing, a gilt was added by hand, which in later years was to wear off. Potters must have had a real struggle before they finally perfected a copper lustre finish that would endure. The gold leaf did not respond well to the heat of the kiln; extra labor was required to apply this by hand in earlier sets.

A "Tea leaf" design with a wavy line and a separate bud was used by Edward Walley over his *Niagara Shape,* which had been registered in 1856. Other potters decorated their white ironstone forms with green bands and a center clover in green.

Photograph 86 shows a rectangular shape trimmed with gold lustre (not copper) in a design very similar to the tea leaf drawing. Powell and Bishop marked these pieces with the year 1876.

By the late 1870s, English potters had perfected a permanent underglaze copper lustre on beautiful dishes that the housewife could use and use without fear that the glow would disappear.

*86. Gold lustre design on a popular style of the 1870s. Footed rectangular shape in the serving pieces accompanied by handled cups with high-walled saucers. Potted by Powell & Bishop in 1876. Collection of Mr. and Mrs. William Horner. Photograph: Dr. Horner.*

I repeat, however, that in the sets first made, this well-known motif was added over shapes that had been already marketed as white ironstone with no added color. Below are some of the shapes I have seen decorated with *Copper Tea Leaf:*

*New York Shape* by J. Clementson
*Portland Shape* by Elsmore & Forster
*Chinese Shape* by Anthony Shaw
*Lily of the Valley* by Anthony Shaw (with lily finial)
*Cable and Ring* by Anthony Shaw
*Peerless* by John Edwards
*Victory* by John Edwards

Through the 1880s, at least twenty Staffordshire manufacturers produced set after set of *Lustre Band and Sprig*. Among them were Henry Burgess, Wedgwood & Co., Alfred Meakin, T. Furnival & Sons, John Edwards, Arthur Wilkinson, Clementson Bros., Johnson Bros., Powell & Bishop and others.

During the same decade, a few American potteries advertised china sets described as "underglaze Lustre Band and Sprig." In 1881, J. & E. Mayer of the well-known Staffordshire family of potters came to America and used their knowledge to open a pottery at Beaver Falls, Pennsylvania. They guaranteed that their copper lustre decorations on white granite were "Indestructible as the Rock of Ages!" Working near the East Liverpool pottery area, the Cartright Brothers also made sets of tea leaf ironstone. I'm sure other native craftsmen must have tried to capture some of the great market for china trimmed in this manner.

Drawn below are A and B, two of the earlier copper motifs, and C, the finished design that was copied on thousands of sets in the eighties.

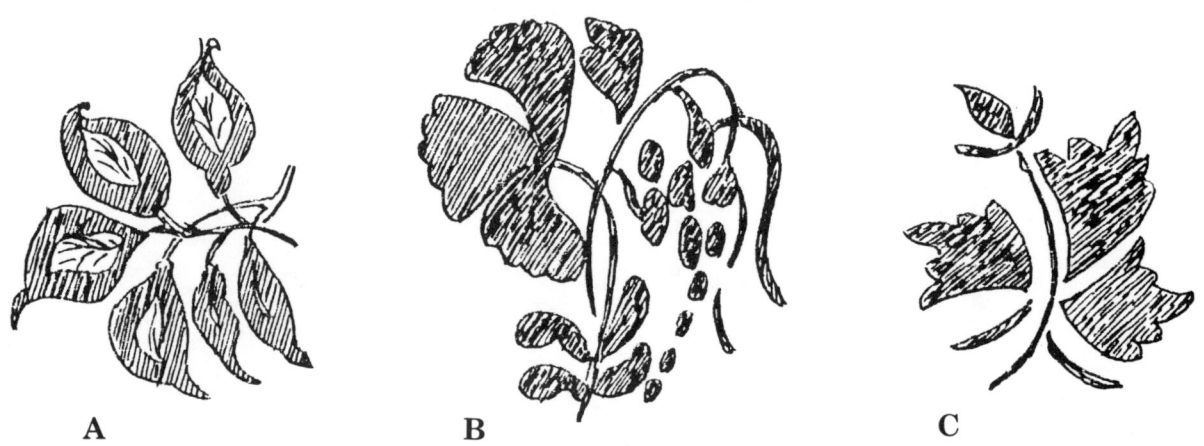

A　　　　　　　　　　B　　　　　　　　　　C

Part of the charm of these dishes is found in the fact that no two designs are exactly alike since all were applied by hand. The design itself has no physical likeness to the leaf of the tea plant but the lines look very familar to me: "Oh, yes, I know I've seen that leaf! I saw it just yesterday when we were searching for wild strawberries." The strawberry stem with its three parts with their serrated edges must have been the original inspiration for the lustre sprig.

Nonetheless, when collectors avidly search for that precious glistening leaf, they'll ask for *Copper Tea Leaf* and others will know exactly what they want. Seen any lately?

87. **CHINESE SHAPE** by Shaw with tea leaf design. Many authorities credit him with the first use of this added decoration. Collection of Mr. and Mrs. William Horner, Delaware. Photograph: Dr. Horner.

88. **NEW YORK SHAPE** piece with dark greenish brown trim by Clementson, left. Oval sugar bowl in light blue trim, accented with cobalt blue, potted 1862, registered by shape in 1856 by Elsmore & Forster, center. CERES shape with chocolate brown color over wheat motif by Elsmore & Forster. All decorated in a similar manner to the later copper tea leaf. Photograph: Blair.

# XVII  Relish Dishes

The drawings in this chapter were gathered together just because I'm fascinated by the varied shapes. And you're a captive audience. Caught the white ironstone fever yet?

When leafing through the photographs in Godden's *Mason's Patent Ironstone China,* I saw where some of the leaf and shell shapes had originated. These unusual dishes were pictured as parts of dessert sets. One dessert set often had three or four original shapes that remind us of the later pickle or relish dishes that were a part of white ironstone dinner sets.

The decoration of some of these small servers had no relation to the design stamped on the bottom. For example, "D" was a leaf shape marked *Sydenham* although the lines are unrelated to *Sydenham* lines. This same dish with little variation has been found marked *Columbia Shape.* Perhaps that is why we are not able to name many of the relish dishes. However, some are clearly stamped or else we recognize the patterns, especially those made in later years.

A collection of these dishes with its variety of shapes can be displayed in a small area. It doesn't crowd you out of the house as much as the larger collections and thus has become quite popular. I'm plotting just how I can have narrow shelves built to show off my relish dishes!

As mentioned elsewhere in this book, ironstone fans use these dishes to serve tossed salad and keep conversation going. It's fun. Of course, they are still used for their original uses too: offering pickles, relishes, nuts and candies.

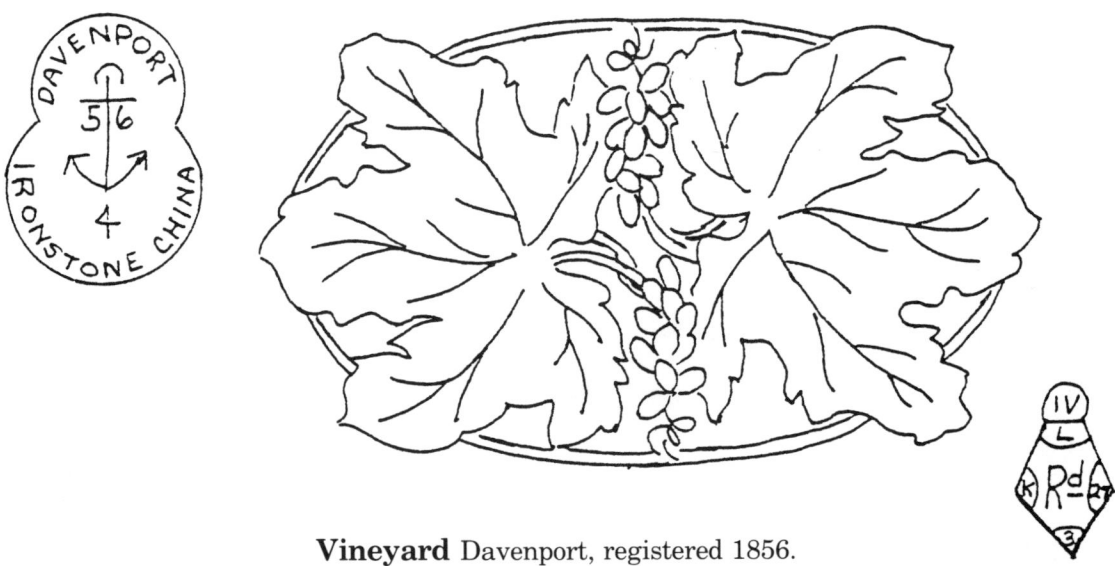

**Vineyard** Davenport, registered 1856.

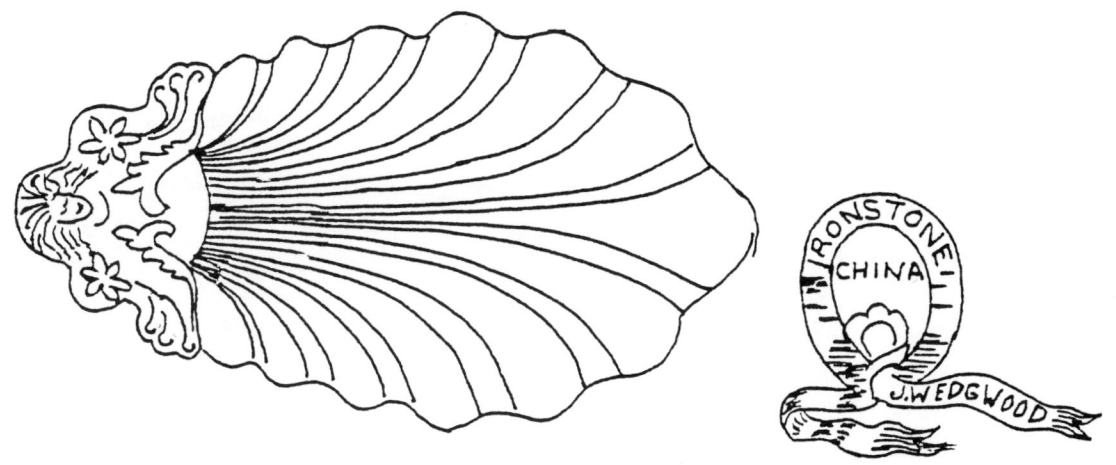

**Early Cameo** J. Wedgwood, Davenport, registered 1848.

**Double Leaf** James Edwards, circa 1848.

JAMES EDWARDS
DALEHALL

CIRCA 1848

J.CLEMENTSON
SHELTON
(IMPRESSED)

**Sydenham or Columbia** This shape was used for the relish dishes sold with these two patterns. This particular dish was made by Clementson.

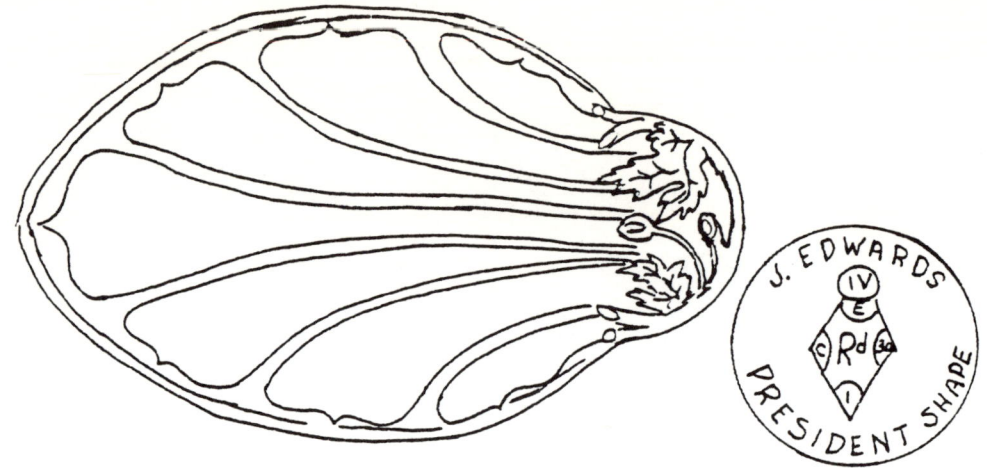

**President Shape** by J. Edwards.

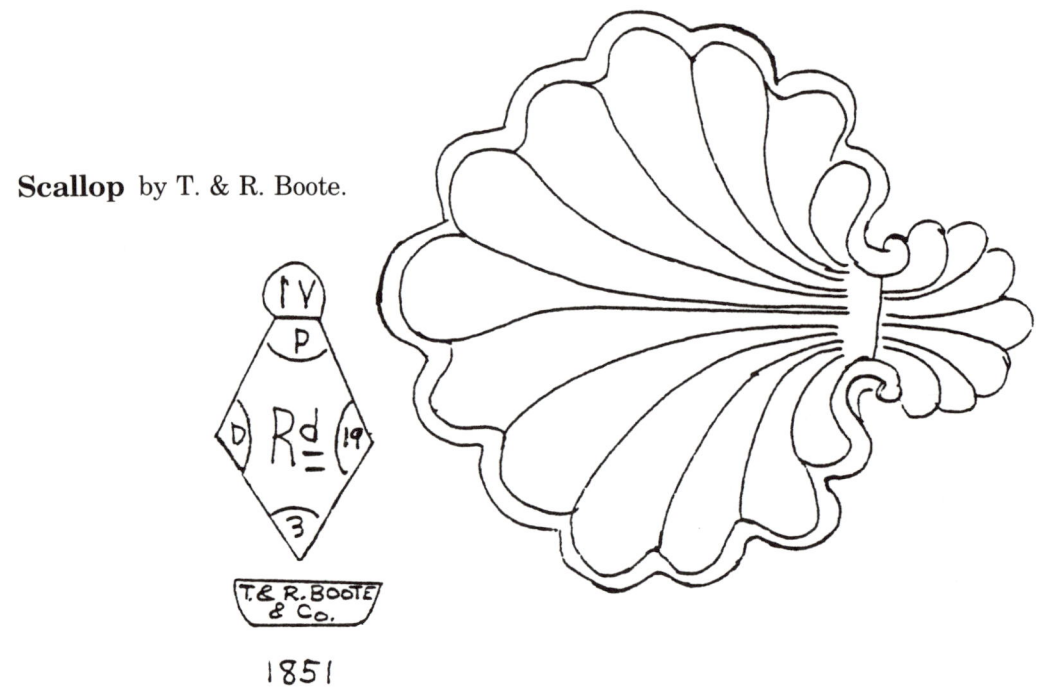

**Scallop** by T. & R. Boote.

1851

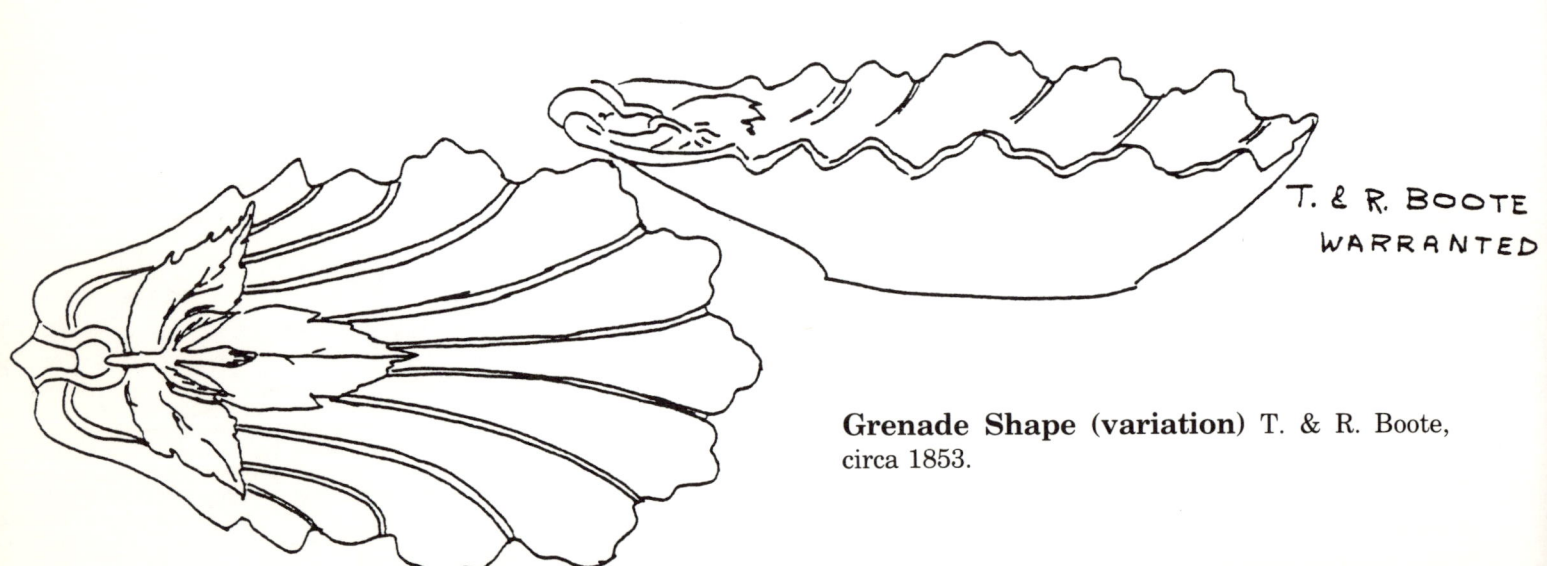

**Grenade Shape (variation)** T. & R. Boote, circa 1853.

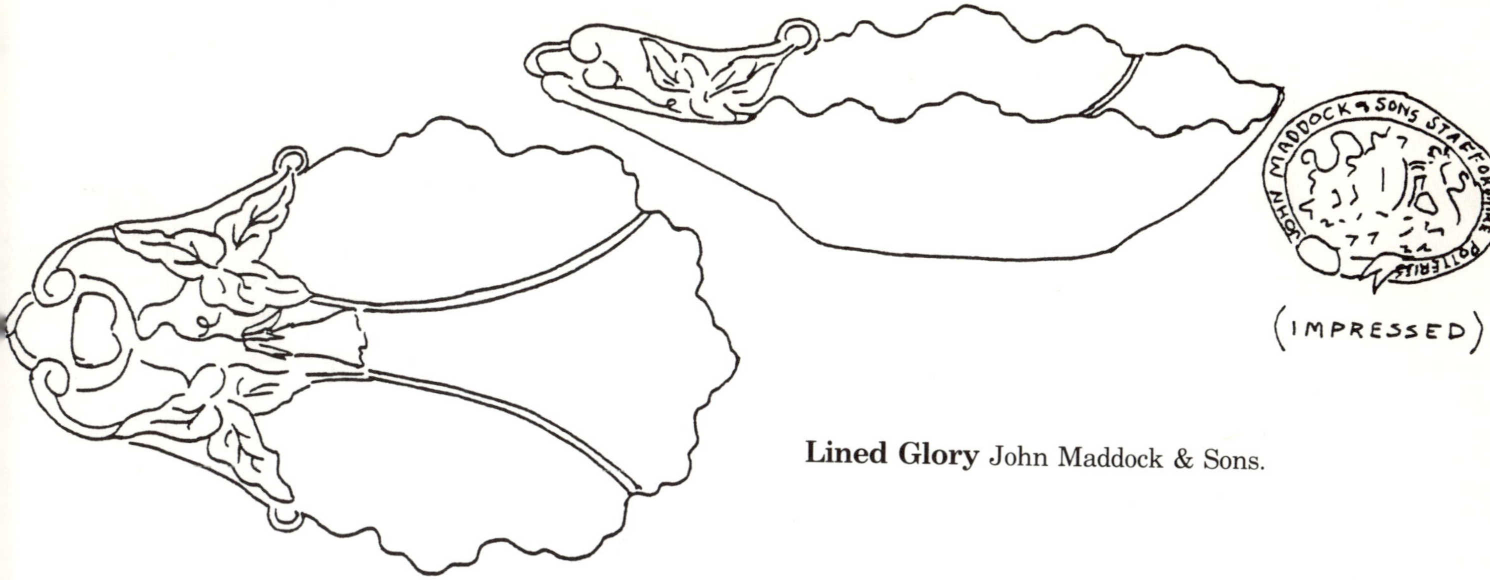

**Lined Glory** John Maddock & Sons.

**Fruit of the Vine** J. & G. Meakin.

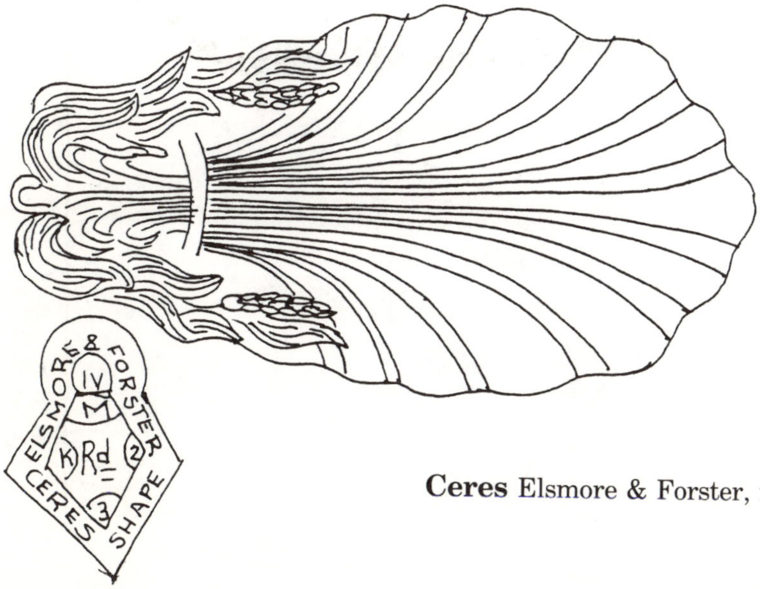

**Ceres** Elsmore & Forster, registered 1859.

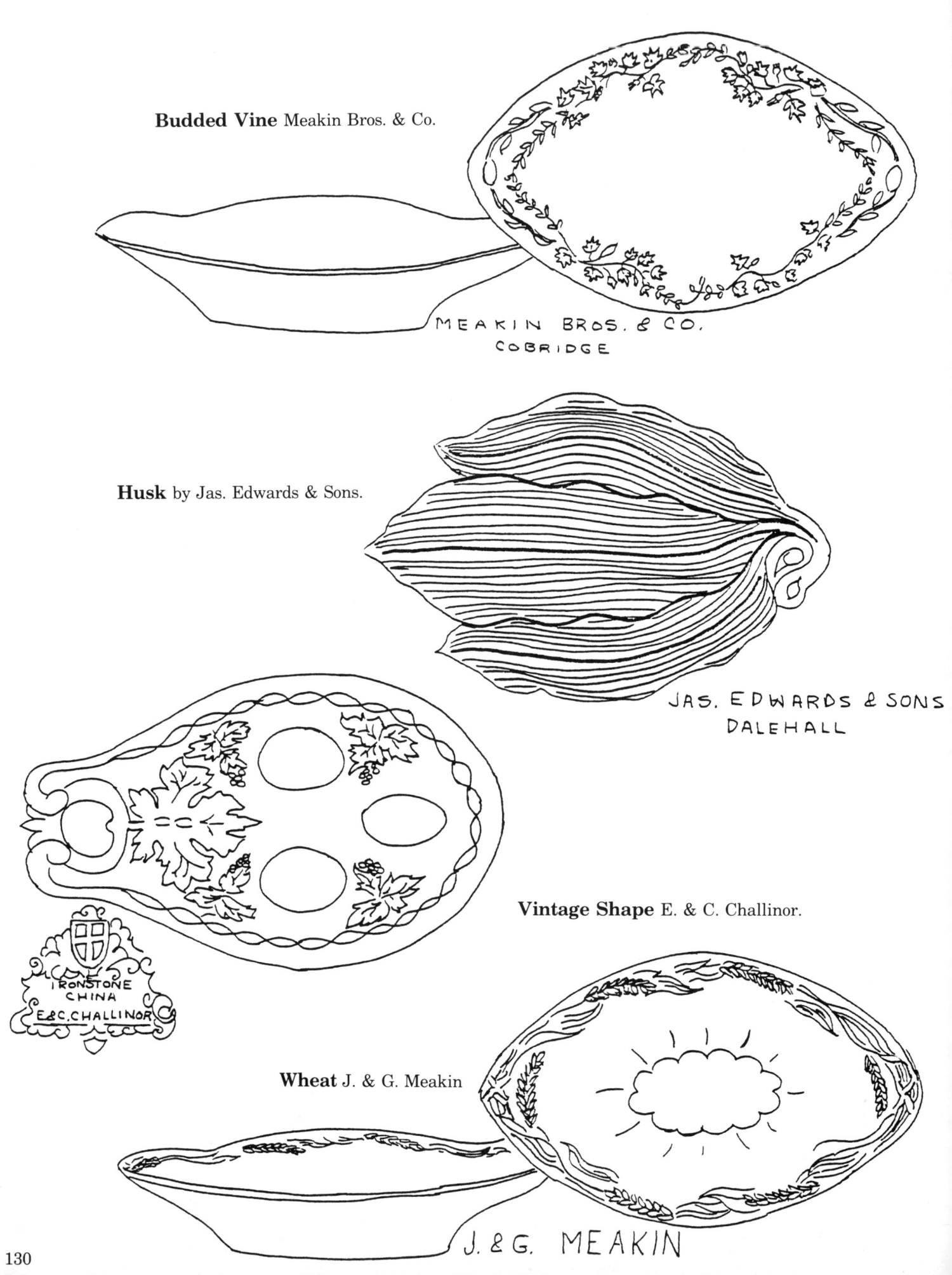

**Budded Vine** Meakin Bros. & Co.

**Husk** by Jas. Edwards & Sons.

**Vintage Shape** E. & C. Challinor.

**Wheat** J. & G. Meakin

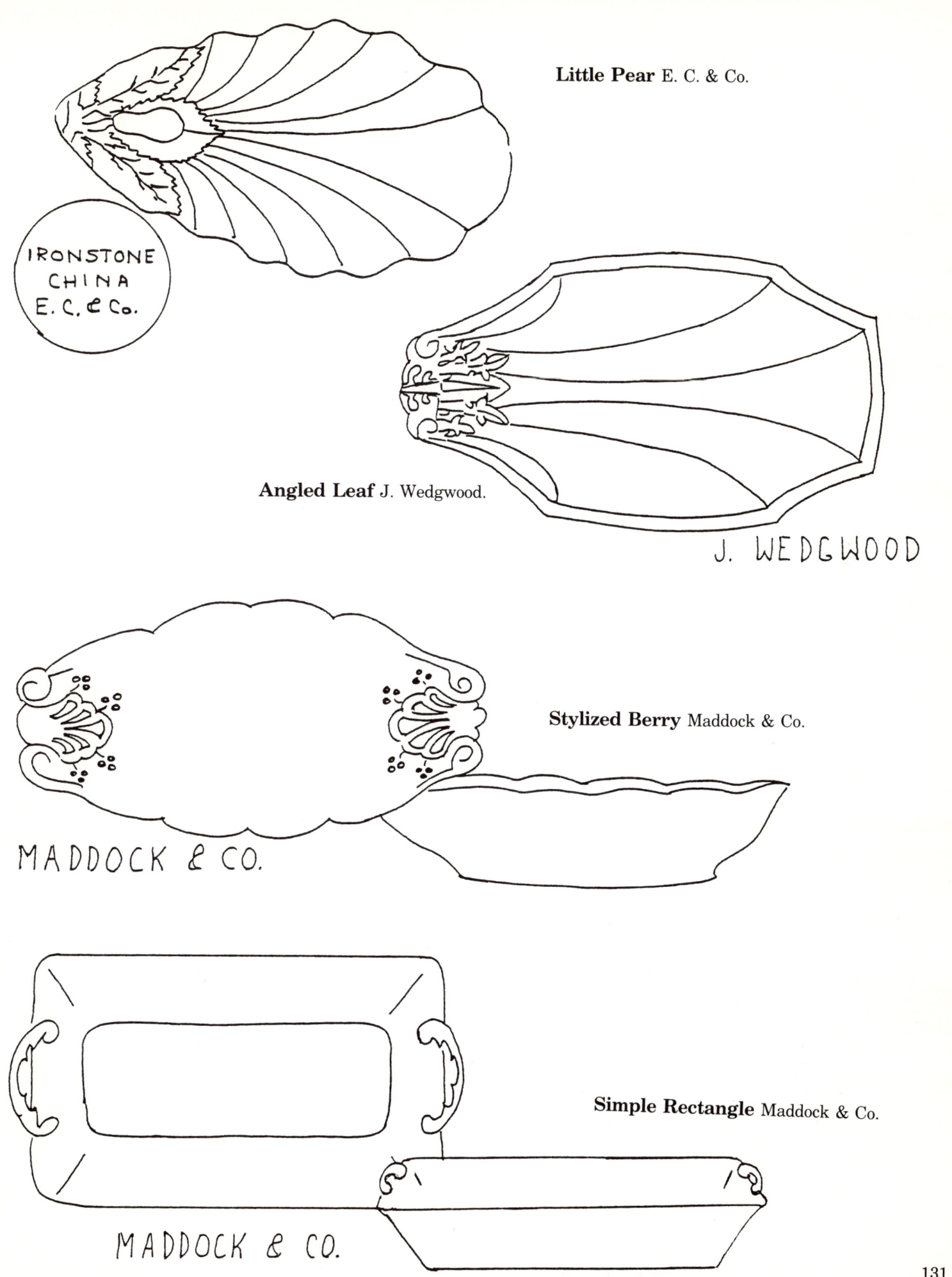

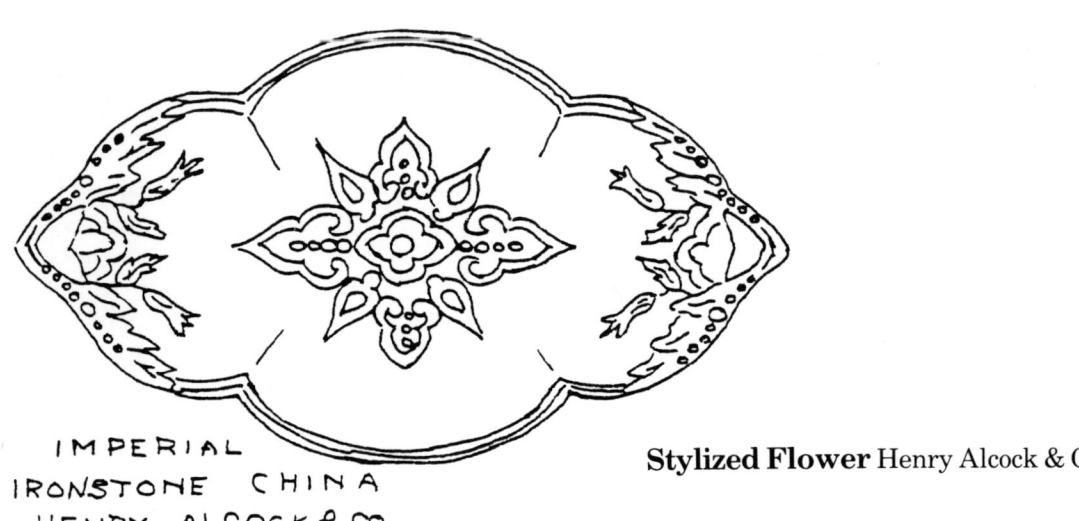

IMPERIAL IRONSTONE CHINA HENRY ALCOCK & CO. after 1861

**Stylized Flower** Henry Alcock & Co. (after 1861).

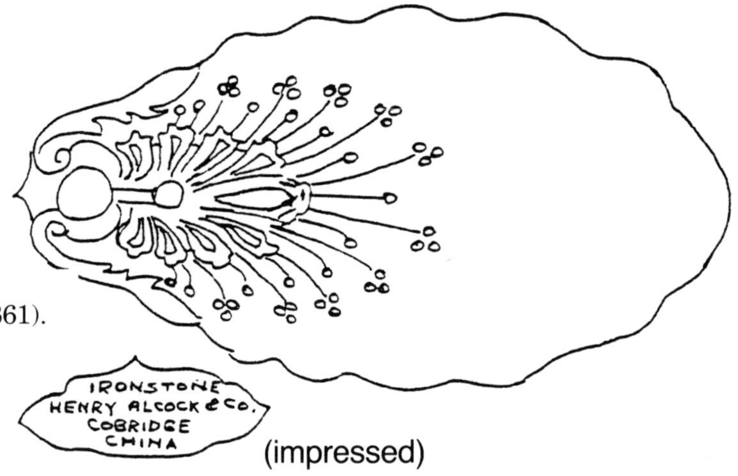

**Floral Ray** Henry Alcock & Co. (after 1861).

IRONSTONE HENRY ALCOCK & CO. COBRIDGE CHINA (impressed)

IRONSTONE CHINA MEAKIN & CO.

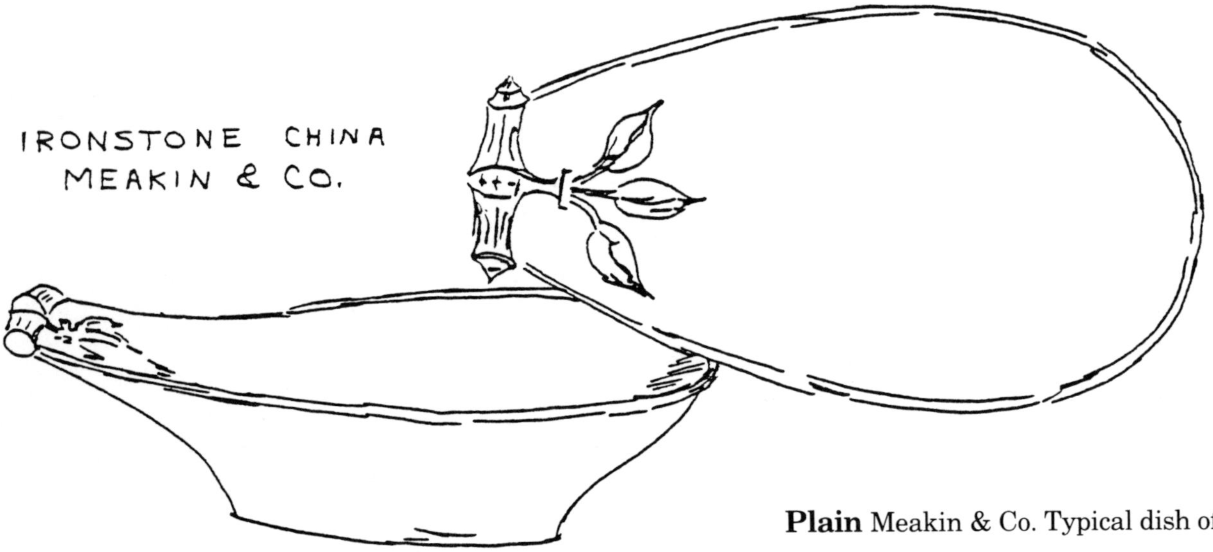

**Plain** Meakin & Co. Typical dish of the 1870s and 1880s.

# XVIII   Native White Ironstone

*They have every material there, equal if not superior to our own for carrying on that manufacture.*

              Josiah Wedgwood, late 1700s.

White graniteware was made in American potteries from about 1860 to 1900. At first, simple patterns and methods were copied from the Staffordshire potters in England. The finer processes, however, were closely guarded secrets kept English generation after English generation. Much American experimentation was necessary.

On the American continent, there were inexhaustible resources for the china maker: endless stores of rich kaolin (the fine white pipe clay first used by the Cherokees), unlimited sources of many other kinds of clay, earths in Alabama, lithomarge in Tennessee, and unknown resources in the ground of the Far West. Now the population was less mobile; ready markets were found in every American city and on the farms that dotted the countryside; and finally, the native potters began in earnest to produce American-made dishes.

When American potters were struggling to capture a portion of the native china market, they were sometimes forced to resort to marking their wares so that the housewife would think she was buying an import. Therefore, we run across marks that confuse us. A few look almost exactly like the Royal Arms, but closer observation aids in the identification. One example of this is a mark stamped by the Glasgow Pottery Co., Trenton, New Jersey, which appears to be the English Arms except that its monogram replaced the quartered decoration within the shield. The old majestic lion reclines just as proudly as ever and the fabulous unicorn prances on. Other marks more subtly implied English origins with anchor, feather, crown, or circled motifs. Old records reveal that some orders for white American table services were specifically requested to be filled in an unmarked condition. This is a little sad for the collector of early American china. I have seen a few pieces that are almost exact copies of the English Gothic-type designs and are not labeled at all. Perhaps they were made by one of the early potteries that produced some native dishes before the last quarter of the nineteenth century.

Jersey City Pottery was founded in 1829. This firm was taken over by Rouse & Turner who, soon after 1850, began to mark whitewares with the English coat of arms in the hope of capturing some of the market used by the English.

In the late 1850s, the now-famous Bennington, Vermont potters of the United States Pottery Co. made gray-white toilet sets that included soap dishes, chamber pots, slop jars, and foot tubs, in addition to the usual bowl and pitcher.

The bodies were thick, not unlike some of the English ironstone. Some of the shapes were related to the lines of the popular *Gothic* and the *Sydenham* designs. Many pieces were decorated with gilt and often had the owner's name emblazoned on one side, revealing the fact that orders were placed ahead of time. In later years this same firm filled orders for large white granite "presentation pitchers" decorated profusely with gilt, colored flowers, and the name of the honored person or firm.

City Pottery, Trenton, was the first company to manufacture white granite in the New Jersey pottery center outside Trenton. This firm received a medal from the New Jersey Agricultural Society for best white graniteware.

First to make ironstone china west of the Alleghenies, John Wyllie and his son left Pittsburgh and moved west to East Liverpool, Ohio. They purchased the two-kiln pottery of Brunt & Hill and re-equipped it for making whiteware in 1874. For seventeen years they made ironstone, some with decorations in full color.

Much American white ironstone is found unmarked. Some were proudly marked and a partial list of those marks and their potters is included at the end of this chapter. No attempt has been made to delve deeply into American ceramics here except to clarify the differences between native and English white ironstone.

At first only the English coat of arms or adaptations of it were included with the potter's initials. Later state coats of arms were used widely in the marks on American-made dishes. Descriptive terms such as "ironstone china," "semi-granite," "white granite china," or "paris white," were sometimes printed with the potter's mark.

By the early 1870s, ceramics in America began to come of age. The silversmiths, the potters of useful crockery, and molders of glassware, had already marketed goods that rivaled similar English products. The chief chinaware manufacturers in America worked around the potting centers near Trenton, New Jersey, and East Liverpool, Ohio. As our country's first centennial approached, a new pride in American-made products increased. The United States government reinforced this feeling by entering on a decade of high tariffs: up to 50 percent on imported ceramic wares. As a result, native potters were challenged to produce china that was acceptable to the American housewife who had always thought, "China to be good must be imported!"

In January 1875 at Philadelphia, seventy representatives of the National Association of Potters of U.S. agreed not to copy patterns from other countries and also agreed to enter exhibits of native work in the Centennial Exhibition the following year.

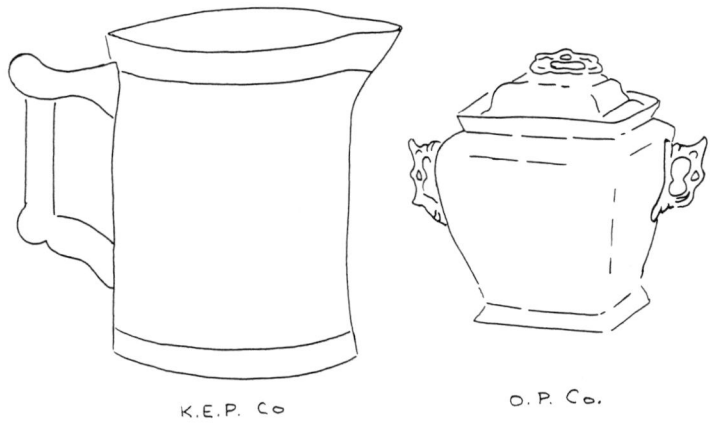
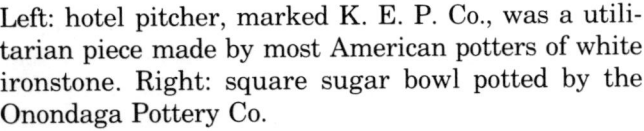

Left: hotel pitcher, marked K. E. P. Co., was a utilitarian piece made by most American potters of white ironstone. Right: square sugar bowl potted by the Onondaga Pottery Co.

Unmarked cup forms were shaped into an invalid feeder (top) and a hand spittoon (below). Grotesque face (or similar masks) circled the hole used to clean a plain, large spittoon made in the States.

Despite the last resolution, the ceramic exhibit was almost hidden and attracted little attention in its corner. Examples of potters' crafts were displayed by the Trenton, Philadelphia, and New York potters but there were no entries from the Ohio firms. The wares attracting some attention were those of the New York City Pottery, Ott & Brewer, and Union Porcelain Works. A white graniteware "Daily Bread" platter was shown by the Trenton Pottery Co.

Another Philadelphia Centennial exhibitor that was noticed was the St. Johns Chinaware Co. from St. Johns, Quebec, located about twenty-three miles southeast of Montreal. This was the first pottery in Canada to concentrate on the production of whiteware. It had begun potting in 1874 under the leadership of Farrars, who had migrated from New England. At first he had difficulty in finding skilled potters who knew how to work with whitewares; finally, he was compelled to employ Staffordshire men for more than half of the work force in his pottery.

The company went bankrupt in 1887 and was eventually bought out by president MacDonald, whose works employed 400 men by the following year. The pottery was closed in 1899, new French owners having found it too difficult to import the clay required for shaping whiteware.

The ironstone made by the St. Johns Stone Chinaware Co. was inexpensive, well-made china, some of which was decorated with gilt and flowers. Some all white dishes I have seen marked by this company were in the *Wheat and Blackberry*, *Wheat* and *Scallop* patterns. St. Johns also potted sets shaped in white ironstone and decorated with blue transfer designs in the Staffordshire manner.

Most of the American sets of white ironstone china were plain with a little design in relief. The English pattern, *Cable and Ring*, was also made by Greenwood Pottery Co., Cook and Hancock, and American Crockery Co. Wheat motifs and rectangular and square shapes were often used. The potters were struggling with the textures of the clay itself, with the purity of the white color, and with the smoothness of the glazes. Their most original contributions are now found in a collection of useful wares: spittons, invalid feeders, milk pans, mush bowls, "pig" bed warmers, foot tubs, wine coolers, nests of square or round servers, etc.

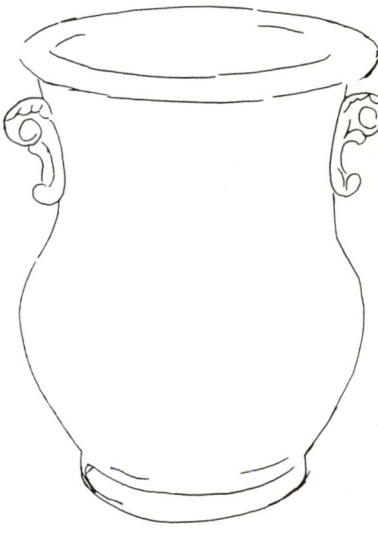

American-made, large rectangular soup tureen, tray, and ladle were potted by the Glasgow Pottery Co. of Trenton, New Jersey, founded in 1863. J. M. & Co. referred to John Moses & Co.

The jardiniere was unmarked as are many of the American-made pieces.

Perhaps the most fascinating collection items formed by the native American potters would be the *Daily Bread Platters*. Almost every firm shaped these oval servers, decorated them with wheat, and varied the wording occasionally. Most slogans begin with "Give Us This Day" on one border and conclude the quote on the opposite side, "Our Daily Bread." Others admonish "Waste Not — Want Not": some advise "Where Reason Rules — The Appetite Obeys." I have seen these platters marked as below:

        T. P. Works (Trenton Pottery Co.)
        J. M. & Co. (Glasgow Pottery Co.)
        M. P. & Co.
        O. P. & Co. (Onondaga Pottery Co.)
        John Wyllie & Son
        St. Johns, P.Q.

I'm sure there were other companies that offered these interesting bread servers. Prices range from twenty to forty dollars according to condition, locality and workmanship. Keep your eyes open for this memorabilia of American ingenuity.

A few pieces of nineteenth century white ironstone in your collection would serve to remind you of the struggle of American craftsmen to figure out how to design, shape, fire and glaze native china. These early ironstone chamber sets, common table settings, and sturdy hotel china helped keep U.S. potters in business. By the turn of the twentieth century some fine china was being produced and the American pottery industry had finally come into its own.

89. *DAILY BREAD PLATTER highly collectible dish made by American potters of white ironstone. Most included a wheat motif as did this one by Onondaga Pottery Co. Owned by James and Doris Walker. Photograph: Blair.*

90. A half-dozen pieces of American-made ironstone, typical of early native potting in white graniteware. Unmarked except for square dish in center bottom which is marked with a printed "91" (probably 1891) over arms circling a monogram in a shield. Photograph: Blair.

93. Unmarked American pieces: Square sugar box and mustard cups decorated with a three-dimensional face similar to GOTHIC CAMEO, Photograph 20. Photograph: Blair.

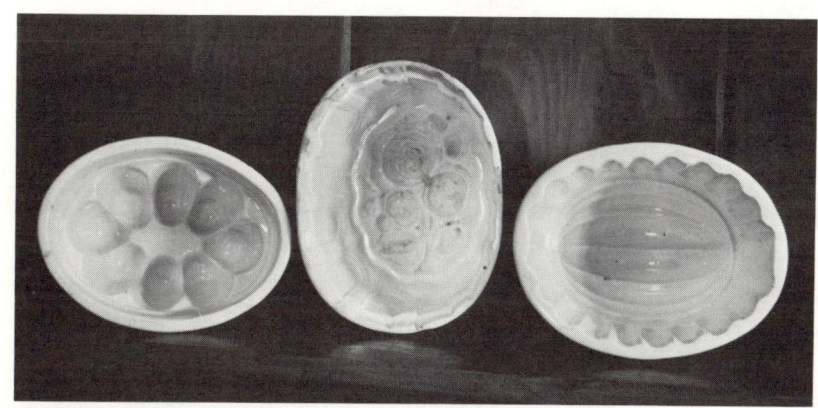

91. Pudding molds, usually unmarked, were often potted by American firms. Owned by the Hoggs in New York. Photograph: Blair.

92. A group of American-made utilitarian pieces. Top: Onondaga Pottery Co., spittoon with colonial profile cameo decoration and another spittoon with gargoyle design. Bottom: unmarked chamber pot, hand spittoon in one piece, hand spittoon in two pieces marked "1866 Nat. Home for Volunteer Soldiers." Collection of Mr. and Mrs. John Black. Photograph: Black.

94. Several American potteries made these melon-ribbed compotes in various sizes. Unmarked.

137

# Partial List of American Potters of White Ironstone

\* Exhibited in the Philadelphia Centennial Exposition of 1876.

| Firm and Location | Marks | Date Founded |
|---|---|---|
| Alpaugh & Magowan<br>Empire Pottery<br>New Jersey | A. & M. | 1884 |
| American China Co.<br>Toronto, Ohio | | 1897 |
| American Crockery Co.<br>Trenton, New Jersey | English arms<br>A.C. Co. | 1876 |
| Anchor Pottery<br>Trenton, New Jersey | Modified English arms with AP monogram in center | 1894 |
| L. B. Beerbower & Co.<br>Elizabeth, New Jersey | STONE CHINA | — |
| Beerbower & Griffin<br>Phoenix Pottery<br>Phoenixville, Pennsylvania | Arms of state of Pennsylvania and in circle initials B. & G. | 1867 |
| Edwin Bennett Pottery Co.<br>Baltimore, Maryland | E.B. Phoenix | 1875 |
| Wm. Brunt Pottery Co. | W.B.P. Co. | 1894 |
| Burgess & Campbell<br>International Pottery Co.<br>New Jersey | | 1879 |
| Burroughs & Mountford<br>Trenton, New Jersey | B. & M. | 1879 |
| \* City Pottery Co.<br>Trenton, New Jersey | Shield<br>C.P. Co. | 1859 |
| Cook & Hancock<br>Crescent Pottery<br>New Jersey | Cook & Hancock | 1881 |
| Coxon & Co.<br>Trenton, New Jersey | Badge with eagle in center and ribbon beneath with name of firm | 1863 |
| Crown Pottery Co.<br>Evansville, Indiana | English arms with C.P.C. monogram in center | 1891 |
| Messrs. Dale & Davis<br>Prospect Hill Pottery<br>Trenton, New Jersey | | 1880 |
| East Liverpool Pottery Co.<br>East Liverpool, Ohio | E.L.P. Co. | 1881 |
| East Trenton Pottery Co.<br>Trenton, New Jersey | E.T.P. Co.<br>New Jersey seal also English arms | White granite by 1888 |

| | | |
|---|---|---|
| * Etruria Pottery<br>Trenton, New Jersey<br>(subsequently Ott & Brewer) | Etruria Pottery | 1863 |
| Fell & Thropp Co.<br>Trenton, New Jersey | English arms<br>F.&T. Co. | — |
| Globe Pottery Co.<br>East Liverpool, Ohio | Globe Pottery Co. | 1881 |
| Goodwin Pottery Co.<br>East Liverpool, Ohio | | 1876 |
| Greenwood Pottery<br>Trenton, New Jersey | G.P. Co.<br>Greenwood China<br>(after 1886) | c 1860 |
| Harker Pottery Co.<br>East Liverpool, Ohio | Horizontal bow<br>with vertical<br>arrow<br>H.P. Co. | 1879 |
| Jersey City Pottery<br>Jersey City, New Jersey<br>(subsequently Rouse & Turner) | | 1829 |
| Knowles, Taylor & Knowles<br>East Liverpool, Ohio | K.T. & K. | 1872 |
| Homer Laughlin & Co.<br>East Liverpool, Ohio | HOMER<br>LAUGHLIN | 1879 |
| * Thomas Maddock & Sons<br>Eagle Pottery<br>Trenton, New Jersey | EAGLE POTTERY | 1869 |
| Maryland Pottery Co.<br>Baltimore, Maryland | Circular eagle<br>MARYLAND<br>POTTERY CO. (seal of<br>Maryland after 1883) | 1881 |
| Mayer Pottery Co.<br>Beaver Falls, Pennsylvania | Square enclosing<br>a circle with<br>WARRANTED STONE<br>CHINA<br>J.&E. MAYER | 1881 |
| Mellor & Co.<br>Cook Pottery Co.<br>New Jersey | MELLOR & CO. | — |
| Mercer Pottery Co.<br>Trenton, New Jersey | Double shield<br>MERCER<br>POTTERY CO. | 1868 |
| Millington & Astbury Pottery<br>Trenton, New Jersey | M.A.P. | 1853<br>Whiteware<br>after 1861 |

| | | | |
|---|---|---|---|
| | Morley & Co.<br>Wellsville Pottery Co. | M. & Co. | 1879 |
| * | Messrs. Morrison & Carr<br>New York City Pottery<br>New York, New York | | 1860 |
| * | John Moses & Co.<br>(Glasgow Pottery Co.)<br>Trenton, New Jersey | Eagle over shield<br>J.M. & Co. | 1863 |
| | New England Pottery Co.<br>East Boston, Massachusetts | Seal of state of<br>Massachusetts from<br>1878 to 1883 | 1854 |
| | Onondaga Pottery Co.<br>Syracuse, New York | Arms of New York<br>O.P. Co. | 1871 |
| | Peoria Pottery Co.<br>Peoria, Illinois | English arms<br>(no initials)<br>WARRANTED | 1873 |
| | Potter's Cooperative Co.<br>East Liverpool, Ohio | DRESDEN | 1876 |
| | Rouse & Turner<br>(formerly Jersey City Pott.)<br>Jersey City, New Jersey | R.&T. | before 1850 |
| * | St. Johns Stone<br>Chinaware Co.<br>St. Johns, Province of<br>Quebec, Canada | English arms<br>ST. JOHNS, P. Q. | 1874 |
| | Steubenville Pottery Co.<br>Steubenville, Ohio | S. P. Co.<br>(others) | 1879 |
| | Trenton Pottery Co.<br>Trenton, New Jersey | T.P. CO. CHINA | 1865 |
| * | Union Pottery Co.<br>New Jersey | | c 1880 |
| | United States Pottery Co.<br>Bennington, Vermont | | 1849 |
| | Vodrey & Brothers | Monogram<br>V over B | 1879 |
| | Wheeling Pottery Co.<br>Wheeling, West Virginia | STONE CHINA | 1879 |
| | Willets Manufacturing Co.<br>Trenton, New Jersey | W.M. Co. | 1879 |
| | John Wyllie & Son<br>Great Western Pottery<br>East Liverpool, Ohio | Double shield of<br>English and U. S.<br>seals<br>J.W. & SON | 1874 |

# XIX  Is It Worth Keeping?

That's what the collector often asks as he looks at a stained, chipped, or cracked piece of ironstone. You can afford to pay a small price for damaged pieces if you think there's a chance of rehabilitating them. The sources for locating these discolored or poorly repaired items are garage sales, country auctions, cellars or attics of old houses, and bottom shelves or dark corners of antique shops.

If a piece has black streaks, rust spots, or if the age cracks appear imbedded with the dust of years, a thorough cleaning may work miracles. (My husband wishes that I were as interested in getting our daily dishes clean as I am in removing the grime from old dishes!) First, try cleaning the whole surface with a non-scratching cleanser such as Bon Ami or Delete. The last product is made by the Drackett Products Company, Cincinnati, Ohio, but I buy it in the local supermarket. It has an added ingredient, oxalic acid, that tackles rust stains. However, follow the directions on the can since this acid is dangerous to the skin and eyes. There are also some rust removers in paste form on the market that do a good job on the rust stains.

Here I have to retract some suggestions that some of you may have read in my first little *White Ironstone* book. Do not — I repeat — do not soak white ironstone or any dish in Clorox or any clorine bleach. It often lightens dark stains but it can also loosen the glaze and ruin the dish. The only time I use Clorox is to remove dirt from a bad crack. I only do this because I figure the dish is already ruined by the disfiguring crack and I might be lucky enough not to start the flaking of the glaze. The first aid I suggest for the dark crack is to immerse the whole piece in undiluted Clorox and boil for five minutes. Remove from the solution and wash thoroughly in warm soapy water. Maybe you'll have a piece you'll be proud to display. Proceed at your own risk!

I have some dishes with little pitted spots where the potter didn't glaze carefully. There's nothing one can do about this but accept it as a natural part of an authentic piece of old white ironstone. After all, these dishes were quickly manufactured to supply the daily serving needs of thousands during the nineteenth century.

Another flaw is called a bull's-eye. Found most often on plates and platters, it is a dark spot, surrounded by white and then a darker ring of stain. The center spot is a break through the tough waterproof glaze and the stain has crept inward to the body of the clay itself. This type of damage cannot be repaired and you must take it into consideration when buying or selling.

If you have located a teapot, sugar bowl or vegetable dish with a finial handle that has been mended clumsily, don't dismiss it too soon if you really like the pattern. Many of the interesting old lids, topped with shapes of fruit, flowers, nuts, or even an animal head couldn't stand the constant handling and the decoration fell off. Since each had doubtless been molded separately and then fastened to the main body before firing in the kiln, this tendency to weaken is understandable. Great grandmother was quite resourceful, however, and often glued or puttied them back on and put the ironstone back to work. At first glance, the yellowed, dirty patching job seems to have ruined the appearance. Study the item carefully to ascertain whether or not a piece is missing. If it's all there, take a chance and buy it — at reduced cost, of course. Hurry home, heat some vinegar on the stove, hang up your coat, and then boil your prize in order to soften the old adhesive. If it's been glued with epoxy glue, you will be unable to loosen the old repair but you are fairly safe since epoxy is a rather modern material. Now, down to work.

Carefully separate the pieces and work and scrape until all the old agent is removed. You may even have to use a knife on the edges. Don't give up. That dish has been around more than one hundred years and isn't called ironstone for no reason at all! Work until the exposed sides of the break are as white as snow. Then wash and dry the surfaces thoroughly. Study fitting them together until you have exactly completed the puzzle. Then glue with a white resin glue such as Titebond. Hold together manually for ten minutes or tape the finial or handle in place with masking or stretchable tape. Do not leave masking tape on for an indefinite time or you'll find you've created a new problem — removing the tape. Usually the pieces will fit so closely together that you'll be unable to see the repair. Now, you've a new item to add to your display in the corner cupboard.

One day, an antique dealer friend called to tell me she'd found a dozen large *Fig* plates for me. I was elated. I dashed to town to see the find. I was crushed. All of them were free of age cracks, chips and bull's-eyes but only two were white. All the rest were an even ugly light brown. I bought the two and sadly left the others. Today, I'd know better.

I kept experimenting, trying all sorts of methods to whiten ironstone that had turned brown from overwork. The materials used had to be harmless to glazes and colored decorations. I finally figured out the puzzle — a puzzle that had already been solved by many people who were interested in reclaiming old china. The process as described below will remove brown stains nine out of ten times. I hope that many white ironstone dishes will be rescued before you toss them out. Here goes!

You'll need a tightly covered holding tank of enamel, crockery, or plastic. I found that an inexpensive plastic garbage can with enough volume so that a large platter, teapots, or tureens could be submerged worked the best. Dishes are less liable to get broken if a plastic container is used. A good location for your tank is a dark corner of your basement or garage if the cats and kids can't find it.

You'll have to secure the whitening solution from a chemical supplier located in your nearest large city. I have found that the smallest amount they will sell is five gallons at approximately eight dollars per gallon. Some people have only been able to secure it in thirty gallon drums. The name of it is commercial strength 35 percent hydrogen peroxide. Covered and tightly sealed in a dark container, peroxide can be kept indefinitely. Place your dishes to soak and remove them as quickly as possible since uncovering slowly weakens the solution. It remains useful for several months, then it must be renewed.

Soak your discolored dishes in the tightly covered solution for one week. Sometimes this is all that is necessary to restore them. More often some brown remains. Use a wooden or a plastic utensil to help lift the items out of the garbage can. Rinse the peroxide off the dishes and dry them with a cloth. Place on a cookie sheet or a broiler pan and put in your oven. Set the temperature at 200 degrees. After fifteen minutes, look at the dishes. Often there will be dark grease oozing out. Wipe this off and return to the oven for another fifteen minutes. Wipe again. Return to oven, turn off heat, let dish cool as oven does. Wash in warm sudsy water and then place in solution another week. Continue to soak and heat until all discoloration is gone. I hope you'll get as excited as I do at the transformation. At least half of my "mint" ironstone has undergone this treatment.

While hydrogen peroxide is not as dangerous as acids are, it is wise to use it with care. Wear long rubber gloves, trying to avoid splashing. If the peroxide contacts your skin, flush with water immediately. It doesn't sting when you are first touched but has a sort of delayed action. Contacted areas burn and turn white for a short period of time. Also, avert your face when removing the cover over the solution. One collector friend of mine realized that the hair around her face had lightened after several weeks of occasionally opening her container of peroxide. Maybe you'd better cover your hair or else start a new style.

Some of the antique dealers that handle white ironstone will also whiten discolored pieces. Since the cost of setting up a tank is expensive and these people are experienced, it may be cheaper for you to hire your cleaning done if you have only a few pieces to be treated.

A few sample prices for cleaning would be: cups, one dollar-fifty to three dollars, chamber pots, eight dollars, gravy boats, four dollars, sauce tureens, five dollars, saucers, one dollar-fifty, plates, (depending on size) one dollar-fifty to three dollars, covered vegetable dishes, depending on size, seven dollars to twelve dollars, creamers, four dollars, sugars, eight dollars, wash bowls, ten dollars, ewers, ten dollars, and teapots, eight dollars to ten dollars. You would have to inquire for costs for cleaning turkey platters or soup tureens. Please remember that these are only my estimates of present costs and are not prices guaranteed by any professional china cleaner.

Often beautiful dishes can be found (in your favorite pattern, of course) that have small chips. It is quite easy to repair these and thus greatly improve the appearance. I secured an ounce of kaolin from a ceramics supplier and the two tubes that make up epoxy glue. Start with a small amount of glue. Using a toothpick to stir, keep adding the kaolin until you are able to shape it with your fingers. Dust your fingers with the kaolin so the epoxy won't stick. If your hands do get sticky, clean them and redust. Force the epoxy putty you have just made into the chip. Make it as nearly like the original as you can. You can use a little lacquer thinner to smooth the final surface. Let the repaired dish harden for several hours. I use the quick-drying paints used for decorating models. Mixing the color for each dish separately is very important since every one is a little different. I was surprised to find that white with a touch of black was most often right. Do your matching by true daylight. You may have to "feather" the paint slightly out onto the dish. It usually takes several coats to complete the job.

You may find it easier to buy a mending kit from Atlas Mineral & Chemicals Division, ESB Incorporated, Dept. G, Mertztown, Pennsylvania 19539. This includes epoxy putty, white finishing resin, glaze, epoxyglass, and other materials plus directions for china repair. A helpful book is written by Laurence Adams Malone. It is entitled *How to Mend Your Treasures*.

You may locate a piece in one of your favorite patterns that lacks a handle, a corner of a spout, or a triangular piece. If a professional repairer can figure out what the missing design should look like, it may be worthwhile hiring the expert. I've found their prices are not high in comparison to the increased value of the dish. Spouts on teapots and coffee pots are especially apt to get damaged since they insist on protruding and humans insist on pushing them toward the back of cupboards. If you want to use your pot for serving hot beverages, you'd be wise to have the spout invisibly glued and glazed by a professional china repairer.

I forgot to mention that you'd better not wash your mended treasures in the dishwasher. I've forgotten a few times and had to re-repair. Oh, well, as our pert next-door neighbor used to say, "What you don't have in your head, you've got in your heels!"

These are the last of my remarks from the Ironstone Preservation Society. So take a second look before you put that white ironstone dish back under the shelf or give it a toss.

95. *Display of octagon-shaped pieces includes* BOOTE'S 1851 OCTAGON, FIG, SYDENHAM, GOTHIC, *and* BALTIC. *White pitchers perch on high shelf. Photograph: LeBel.*

# XX  Fun with White Ironstone

Now, this chapter is going to concern that intangible, unexplainable urge that finally turns a simple admirer into an insatiable collector. Of white ironstone, that is. In keeping with that spirit, here's a copy of an epitaph found in a country church yard.

### On an Old Woman, who kept an Earthenware Shop

Beneath this ftone lies Katherine Gray,
Chang'd from a bufy life to lifelefs clay.
  By earth and clay fhe got her pelf,
  And now fhe's turned to earth herfelf.
  Ye weeping friends, let me advife,
  Abate your grief, and dry your eyes;
  For what avails a flood of tears?
  Who knows but in a run of years,
  In fome tall pitcher, or broad pan,
  She in her fhop may be again.

Enough said. Now down to collecting. Long ago we bought a large white sugar bowl for my husband because our little one was "always empty." The new one held nearly five cups of sugar and soon served us daily.

A few weeks later my husband remarked, "I saw a little covered dish that matches my sugar bowl, but the dealer wants ten dollars for it." I happened to walk past the same window and there it sat – unstained, unchipped and glaringly white – a covered oval soap dish. A few days later I was suddenly struck with a thought, "That dish would make an excellent butter dish to use with the sugar bowl." Now we had our excuse. My husband tucked an old local milk bottle, which some strange people have taken to collecting, under his arm and went off to swap. We now use our eight-dollar butter dish daily.

My daughter, who was showing symptoms of the onset of the collecting disease, located the matching round covered tureen about eleven inches in diameter in a shop for twenty dollars. That was too expensive. We didn't need it either.

Once in a while on a warm sunny Saturday in summer it happens that four or five rural auctions are scheduled. Now it's a challenge to figure out which one will have a hungry crowd of tourists in a holiday spending mood, which one will have so many dealers that a mere home-hoarder can't compete, or which one will have just a few collectibles (the ones you want) but not enough to attract much competition. The best idea is to come early, look over the goodies, and decide if it's worth while to wait. Naturally you can't do this at all locations at once. There might be a couple of garage sales planned for the day, too. Some of these Saturdays are a complete waste of time, but an occasional successful day really gets you hooked. Now, to continue my tale.

One weekend we went to a barn sale set up to dispose of odds and ends that hadn't been sold at a previous sale. We picked up a box or two of various curiosities and then stopped about noon at an auction which was moderately swinging along. A little disappointed, we saw that the merchandise was just used furniture, nothing old. But the sun was shining, the people were friendly, no one was sitting on an old studio couch, there was a friendly collie dog nearby begging for the last bite of anybody's hot dog. We decided to just rest and enjoy the happy crowd. In about ten minutes a plain ironstone pitcher was offered and no one was particularly anxious to buy it. At, "Two dollars!" my husband raised his hand and got a quick change-of-pace, "Sold!" When we got our purchase to the car we were amazed. It exactly matched his sugar bowl and newly-christened butter dish! You've probably guessed by now that somebody finally bought the large round tureen that matched! We named the pattern *Simplicity* and it served us regularly. Now, our son's family uses it each day.

Through the months that followed I located pieces at house and auction sales, borrowed from friends and antique shops, delighted in ironstone gifts from family and friends. Even damaged pieces and "widowed" dishes added to my knowledge. I read about how the English pottery businesses were carried on during the end of the eighteenth century through the early nineteenth century. I couldn't read up on white ironstone because no one had written extensively on this subject. An occasional short magazine article increased my interest. Pauline Meissen-Helter had listed verbal descriptions of some patterns on a few mimeographed pages. These helped me to identify some dishes.

I compiled all the information I had found, limited though it was and published a small handbook in 1974, entitled *White Ironstone*. I hoped to use this to locate more facts, contact other collectors, and find out if people really were interested in the subject. It was fun to hear from the readers by letter and phone and glean new ideas on the topic. I filed away addresses, sketches, word pictures, price quotes, snapshots – all great propaganda.

We planned tours all over the Northeast and visited collectors' homes and shops that handled white ironstone. What good hosts and hostesses we met – people so enthusiastic about their prizes that they could hardly wait to point to them. It was exciting to see so many similar arrangements in homes hundreds of miles apart. Miniature sets peered down from high safe shelves, hutches were arranged in spotless white with a few colored glass accents, tea was poured from white ironstone teapots and sipped from handleless cups.

People from nearby and people from hundreds of miles away began to drop in, each carrying some finds "that I just thought you'd like to see." No amount of effort seemed to be too great as they helped me in my quest for more knowledge about white ironstone. This book is a result of all that cooperation.

Wherever I traveled I learned to watch for homes that might house ironstone. If there was an ox yoke on the garage wall or an old lantern outside the kitchen entrance or a farm bell near the back door, I'd begin to plot just how to find out if there was any ironstone within. I needn't have plotted so much for most people were eager to show me their row of white sugar bowls or their great soup tureen crowded with zinnias, and they even became enthusiastic about letting me help dig in the attic or cellar. It was fun to find related pieces and exclaim, "Oh, that's how the *President* cover looks!" or "That's a design I've never seen!"

One Western reader wrote, "Darn grandma for giving me that first white ironstone platter. Now, I'm hooked." White ironstone hates not to be used. If the original use doesn't fit in with today's way of life, our creative collectors find new ways to put their whiteware to work.

On one trip, my daughter whispered, "Be sure to visit the bathroom." Yes, there was the whole toilet set in *Fig* arranged so beautifully around the room. Outside another bathroom door was an arrangement of chamber pot covers anchored with plate hangers — very appropriate, I thought. Other people have gathered related shapes from the older octagonal patterns together and arranged them compatibly as in Photographs 96 and 97.

*96. PRESIDENT soap dish by J. Edwards, pitcher by John Alcock, and bowl by R. Beswick form a pleasing arrangement. Collection of Mr. and Mrs. John Black. Photograph: Black.*

*97. Octagonal shapes from four different potters decorate a bedroom corner. Photograph: Blair.*

I applaud the New York lady who wrote that she displays white ironstone covers, with their intricately molded fruit and flower finials, on a plate rail around the walls of her kitchen. Another serves tossed salad in her relish and pickle dishes, adding both nourishment and conversation to her table. Shaped like boats, shells, or leaves, the same dishes can be used on coffee tables or stands to hold nuts or candy.

Those handleless cups with their deep saucers? Just once I've tried serving my after-dinner coffee in them. The cups were too hot to hold and nobody was willing to turn back the years and drink out of the saucers. My husband vetoed that practice emphatically. I stirred up my imagination. The large sixteen ounce cups are now used to serve a generous amount of chowder or stew, house a large sundae with all its gooey glory, or march in a buffet row holding pickles, olives and celery.

Plants and flowers adapt well to ironstone containers. Our florist tells us that he makes up more growing dish gardens in dishes brought in by customers than those receptacles he offers for sale. Moreover, earth doesn't seem to stain this tough ware and some people even think that soil improves the color and lessens age cracks. I just don't know. Vines like ivy or philodendron drape gracefully from a gravy boat or the bottom of a sauce boat, or a dish garden can be arranged in the bottom half of a tureen that has been separated from its cover. If you've been fortunate enough to locate a clean-lined jardiniere you might crowd it generously with large branches of crab apple or lilacs in spring; with dried sorghum, teasel, milk weeds or cattail in a fall arrangement next to the hearth; or set a large Boston fern, pot and all, down inside so only the long green fronds arch evenly up and around the large white container. Let's not forget the appeal of bright fruit overflowing a compote on a coffee table or side board.

98. *Plain lines of compote complement the pure lines of a jardiniere potted by Alfred Meakin after 1891.*

It is quite easy to gather enough plain pieces of white ironstone in dinner plates, large shallow soup dishes, and a few handleless cups with saucers. Then to complete the setting, use your favorite design in the large serving dishes. Another acquaintance sticks simply to the plain whiteware adding the graceful oval side dishes, pitchers, large oval vegetable servers, and a floral centerpiece arranged in an octagonal compote. She feels free to use her dishwasher because the old ware is even tougher and less liable to chip than the new "unbreakable, dishwasher proof" services now being produced.

There are some patterns that can be combined to make a harmonious set. The several *Lily of the Valley* motifs and the *Hyacinth* pattern both have the same long tenuous shards and bell-like flowers. Similar wheat patterns can be combined: our supper plates in wheat are the old *Ceres* pattern while our soup plates were potted by Meakin. No guest really notices unless he counts the heads of wheat in the borders.

Only once have I seen a true punch bowl in white ironstone. It holds six quarts and was potted by the firm of Francis Morley, sometime between 1845 and 1858. I can just imagine the proud host beaming over this amazing receptacle at a holiday gathering, can't you? Study Photograph 99 well. You may never see such a piece again.

*99. Hard-to-find, six-quart punch bowl was potted by Francis Morley between 1845 and 1858. Collectors are Mr. and Mrs. John Black. Photograph: Black.*

*100. NEW YORK SHAPE dishes by Clementson. Photograph: LeBel.*

If you entertain small groups, I hope you'll be fortunate enough to locate a syllabub bowl which holds about three-and-one-half quarts. Ring it with the little pedestaled toddy cups and fill it with your favorite beverage. Maybe you'd like to try the following recipe for "country syllabub" as written by Miss Eliza Leslie in 1848 in her book, *Directions for Cookery in Its Various Branches:*

> Mix a half a pound of white sugar with a pint of fine cider, or of white wine, and grate in a nutmeg. Prepare them in a large bowl, just before milking time. Then let it be taken to the cow, and have about three pints milked into it, stirring occasionally with a spoon. Let it be eaten before the froth subsides.

One young housewife employs her ironstone washbowl to serve her punch. At Yuletide she balances it above evergreens and red velvet cherries; her guests drink from handleless tea cups. She refills her very original punch bowl with refreshment mixed in and poured from the graceful tall ewer that matches the bowl.

When I drop in on you some day, I'll admire your ironstone pitchers hung on wooden pegs, that African violet nestled in an old handleless cup, and your fried chicken will be more delicious lifted from a great ironstone platter! Don't you dare relegate these treasures to the back of the cupboard or the loneliness of an attic corner. Use 'em!

Used on white ironstone, the motifs of grains, fruits, berries, meadow flowers and lush vines may have been designed to please the cottage dwellers or decorate the tables of farm families. Three dimensional finials of ripe fruits, nuts, ears of corn, bursting seed pods and gourds symbolized fertile soil and productive gardens and fields.

Somehow, today some of this aura of plenteous harvest is a connotation of the sturdy ironstone. We envision mounds of fluffy potatoes heaped in large vegetable dishes, savory stews arranged on great white platters, roomy two-quart milk pitchers that really pour, homemade relishes and jams filling boat or leaf-shaped servers, and of course, homemade vegetable soup or corn chowder to be ladled out of great tureens. We daydream of crisp homegrown farm products, the aroma of fresh baked bread, plates of sliced tomatoes, and waving fields of grain and think that these solid, durable dishes can somehow bring back those departed days. Personally, I think we only want the memories – not the drafty houses, hours of backbreaking labor, or hours of preparation for large family meals. But a slice of homemade bread would taste good, wouldn't it?

The popularity of country life has swung full circle in the last hundred years. Farmers used to look forward to the day when they could leave the homestead and the hard work and move to town. Today, the city dwellers long to vacation or retire in the good country air. The epithet "thresher's china" has been exchanged for the charm of those "beautiful blue-white dishes" that great grandma used to feed her family as they gathered around her laden table. We agree – they are beautiful blue-white dishes.

# XXI  In Conclusion

What collector can ever really conclude? Someone calls or brings a new shape for me to study. Across a thousand miles comes a photograph.

Imagine how excited I was when a lady told me she'd found a large serving dish shaped just like the *Scallop* relish dish on page 128. Lately, I've been plotting just how I can get four small *Scallop* dishes together (from four different collections) to pose for a picture with that big *Scallop* server.

Then John Black mailed me more negatives of some unusual finds. Take a peek at what developed.

I could keep on going but this book has to end. I suspect we'll keep on watching for that perfect piece that should join our other treasures.

May the lure of collecting white ironstone be a real challenge to you.

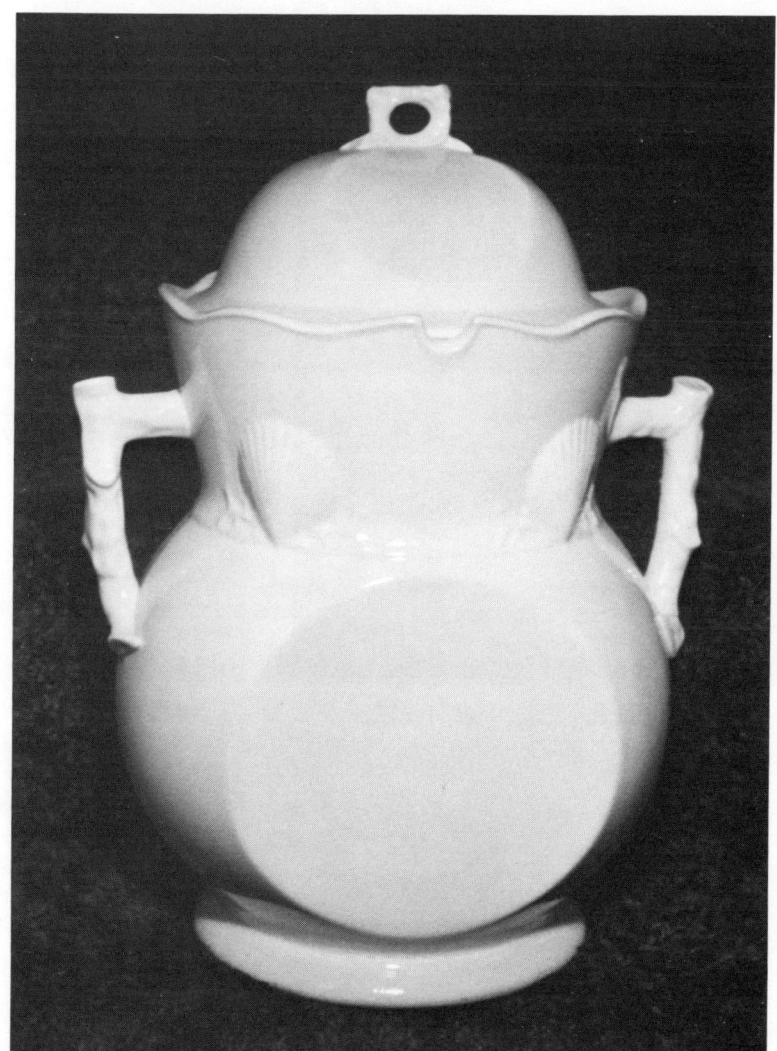

*101. Large unmarked cooler or storage jar is quite unique with its branch handles and shell decoration. Probably potted in America. Photograph: Black.*

102. This unusual plate is kept warm by hot water poured through the side spout. The word "ironstone" can be read in the impressed mark but the other words are indecipherable. Probably of English origin. Photograph: Black.

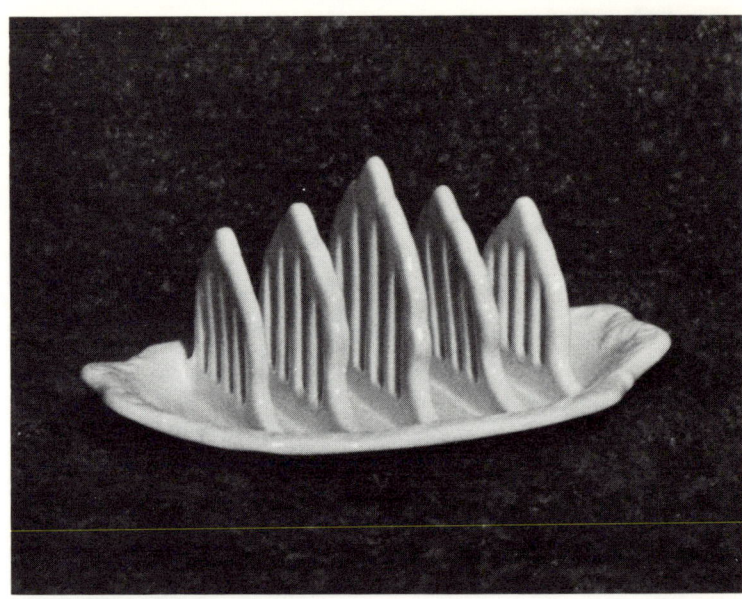

104. Unmarked toast holder graced a breakfast table in the nineteenth century. Photograph: Black.

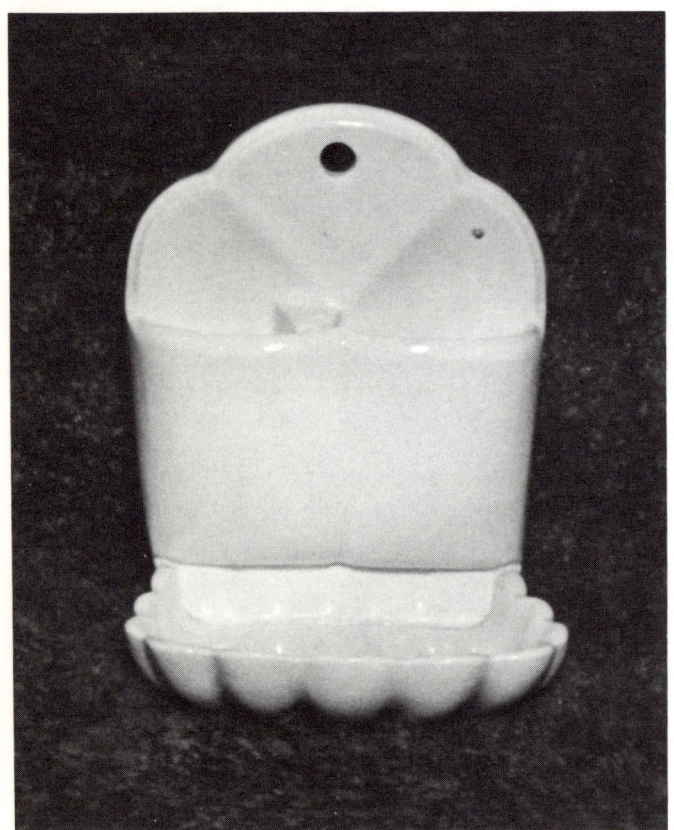

103. Very different indeed is this wall holder for both toothbrushes and soap. Unmarked. Photograph: Black.

105. A wonderful find is this NEW YORK SHAPE chocolate pot located by the Blacks. Just had to show you. Photograph: Black.

# Bibliography

Barber, Edwin Atlee. *Marks of American Potters*. Reprint. Southampton, New York: Cracker Barrel Press, 1968.

Barber, Edwin Atlee. *Pottery and Porcelain of the United States*. New York: G.P. Putnam's Sons, 1893.

Burton, William, F. CS. *A History of English Earthenware and Stoneware*. London: Cassell & Co. Ltd., 1904.

Chaffers, William. *Marks and Monograms on Pottery and Porcelain*. London: Bickers & Son, 1876.

Church, Arthur H. *English Earthenware Made During the 17th and 18th Century*. Revised Edition. London: Wyman and Sons, 1904.

Cole, Ann Kilborn. *How to Collect the New Antiques*. New York: David McKay Co., Inc., 1966.

Drepperd, Carl. *The Primer of American Antiques*. Garden City, New York: Doubleday & Co., Inc., 1944.

Earle, Alice Morse. *China Collecting in America*. New York: Empire State Book Co., 1924.

Eberlein and Ramsdell. *The Practical Book of Chinaware*. Philadelphia and New York: J. B. Lippincott Co., 1925.

Godden, Geoffrey. *Antique Glass and China*. New York: Castle Books, 1966.

Godden, Geoffrey A. F. R. S. A. *Encyclopaedia of British Pottery and Porcelain Marks*. New York: Crown Publishers, Inc., 1964.

Godden, Geoffrey. *The Illustrated Guide to Mason's Patent Ironstone China*. New York: Praeger Publishers, Inc., 1971.

Graham II, John Meredith and Wedgwood, Hensleigh Cecil. *Wedgwood*. New York: The Tudor Publishing Co., 1948.

Hayden, Arthur. *Chats on English China*. London: T. Fisher Unwin Ltd., 1904.

Hughes, Bernard and Therle. *Encyclopedia of English Ceramics*. London: Lutterworth Press, 1956.

Kamm, Minnie Watson. *Old China*. Grosse Pointe, Mich.: Kamm Publications, 1951.

Klamkin, Marian. *American Patriotic and Political China*. New York: Charles Scribners & Sons, 1973.

Little, W.L. *Staffordshire Blue*. New York: Crown Publishers, Inc., 1969.

Mankowitz, Wolf and Haggar, Reginald. *Concise Encyclopedia of English Pottery and Porcelain*. New York: Hawthorn Books, Inc., 1957.

McClinton, Katherine Morrison. *A Handbook of Popular Antiques*. Reprint. New York: Random House, 1965. Distr. by Crown Pub., Inc.

McClinton, Katherine Morrison. *Antiques, Past and Present*. New York: Clarkson N. Potter, Inc., 1971.

Moore, N. Hudson. *The Old China Book*. New York: Tudor Publishing Co., 1903.

Nelson, Glenn. *Ceramics*. New York: Holt, Rinehart, and Winston, Inc., 1971.

Raycraft, Donald R. *Early American Folk & Country Antiques*. Vermont, Japan: Charles E. Tuttle Co., Inc., 1971.

Spargo, John. *Early American Pottery and China*. Reprint. New York: Garden City Pub. Co., Inc., 1948.

*Magazines*

"American Ceramic and the Philadelphia Exhibition." *Antiques,* July 1976, pp. 146-158.

Collard, Elizabeth. "The St. Johns Stone Chinaware Company." *Antiques,* October 1976, pp. 800-805.

Meissen-Helter, Pauline. "What Is Ironstone?" Unpublished.

Rainwater, Dorothy T. "Spoon Warmers," *Spinning Wheel,* October 1977, p. 35.

# Index

Acorn, 80
Adam's Scallop, 37, 42
Adriatic Shape, 59
Alternate Octagon, 87, 147
Angled Leaf, 131
Arbor Vine, 84
Arched Forget-Me-Not, 94
Athena Shape, 105, 106
Athenia, 106
Athens Shape, 106, 107
Atlantic Shape A, 18, 20, 59, 67
Atlantic Shape B, 68
Atlantic Shape C, 68

Baltic Shape, 55, 144
Basketweave, 120
Basketweave with Band, 120
Bellflower, 98
Bell Tracery, 102
Berlin Swirl, 39
Block Optic, 114
Boote's 1851 Octagon, 48, 49, 51, 58, 144
Boote's 1851 Round, 56
Bordered Fuchsia, 91, 97
Bordered Hyacinth, 100
Bow and Tassel, 117
Bow Knot, 113
Budded Vine, 109, 112, 130

Cable and Ring, 109, 115, 124, 135
Canada, 76
Ceres Shape, 20, 21, 33, 34, 36, 71, 72, 122, 125, 129, 149
Cherry Scroll, 113
Chinese Shape, 59, 60, 67, 85, 91, 124, 125
Citron Shape, 80
Columbia Shape, 18, 50, 53, 54, 85, 86, 127
Cone on Fern, 41
Cone with Leaves, 86, 92
Corn and Oats, 8, 26, 70
Copper Tea Leaf, 122-125
Curved Gothic, 38
Curved Rectangle, 114

Daily Bread Platters, 136
Dallas Shape, 55
Desoto Shape, 60
Diamond and Thumbprint, 110
Double Groove, 86
Double Leaf, 127
Double Panel, 112
Double Sydenham, 56
Dove, 110
Dover Shape, 105
Draped Leaf (A), 82
Draped Leaf (B), 82, 119
Draped Leaf (C), 82
Draped Leaf (D), 82

Eagle, 109, 110
Early Cameo, 16, 127
Erie Shape, 59

Fig, 20, 26, 34, 37, 46, 144, 147
Fleur-de-Lis with Leaf, 87
Flora, 93
Flora Shape, 93
Floral Ray, 132
Flower Garden Border, 121
Fluted Pearl, 9, 18, 36, 37, 39
Forget-Me-Not, 93
Framed Leaf, 81
Fruit Garden, 91, 102
Fruit of the Vine, 129
Fuchsia, 91, 95, 96
Fuchsia with Band, 121
Full-Ribbed, 36, 105

Garden Sprig, 94
Garibaldi Shape, 65
Gentle Square, 114
Girard Shape, 64
Gooseberry, 84
Gothic, 16, 18, 19, 23, 37, 38, 133, 144
Gothic Cameo, 44, 137
Gothic Rose, 44
Gourd, 32, 87

Grape and Medallion, 84
Grape Clusters, 109, 111, 112
Grape Clusters with Chain, 109, 112
Grape Octagon, 45, 58
Greek Key, 107
Grenade Shape, 59, 60, 82, 128

Hanging Arch, 79
Have — Shape, 74, 75
Holly (A), 83
Holly (B), 83
Holly (C), 83
Huron Shape, 61
Husk, 130
Hyacinth, 86, 91, 99, 149

Ivy Wreath, 89

Jumbo, 110, 111

Kansas Shape, 18, 59

LaFayette Shape, 18, 59, 63
Laurel, 91, 96
Laurel Wreath, 21, 106, 108
Leaf and Crossed Ribbon, 81
Leaf Fan, 89, 90
Lily of the Valley (A), 99, 101, 149
Lily of the Valley (B), 101
Lily Pad, 88
Lily Shape, 96
Line Trim, 23, 37, 42
Lined Glory, 129
Lion's Head, 109, 113
Little Pear, 131
Little Scroll, 89, 122, 125
Little Palm, 113
Little Western, 101
Long Octagon, 45
Loop and Dot, 85
Loop and Line, 90

Meadow Bouquet, 94
Medici, 108
Memnon Shape, 65
Mississippi Shape, 55
Mitered Block, 114
Montpelier Shape, 18, 59
Morning Glory, 21, 34, 91, 93
Moss Rose, 91, 95

New York Shape, 18, 59, 66, 123, 125, 149, 152
Niagara Shape, 64, 123
Nosegay, 96
Nut with Bud, 89

Olympic Shape, 106

Panelled Grape, 86
Panelled Lily, 57
Paris Shape, 18, 59, 65
Peerless, 124
Persia Shape, 65
Piecrust, 117
Plain, Frontispiece, 118, 119, 132, 148
Plain Uplift, 109, 118
Pomegranate, 85, 86
Portland Shape, 64, 122, 124
Potomac Shape, 80
Prairie Flowers, 73, 74
Prairie Shape, 73
President Shape, 18, 34, 52, 54, 65, 128, 147
Prize Bloom, 37, 47
Prize Puritan, 37, 41

Ribbed Berry, 104
Ribbed Bud, 104
Ribbed Chain, 103, 104
Ribbed Raspberry with Bloom, 103
Rolling Star, 40
Rose Bud, 18, 23, 40, 91

St. Louis Shape, 18, 61
Scallop, 128, 135, 151
Scalloped Decagon, 37, 43, 119
Scotia, 23, 73, 75
Scrolled Border, 88
Seashore Shape, 111
Seine, 116
Senate, 117
Sharon Arch, 26, 33, 79
Shaw's Lily of the Valley, 91, 100, 101, 124
Shaw's Spray, 88
Simple Rectangle, 131
Simplicity, 116, 143, 144, 146
Split Pod, 47
Square Melon-Ribbed, 119
Square Ridged, 114
Stafford Shape, 59
Star Flower, 92
Stylized Berry, 131
Stylized Flower, 132
Sydenham Shape, 18, 20, 33-35, 48-58, 59, 126, 127, 133, 144

Tiny Oak and Acorn, 81
Tracery, 120, 121
Trent Shape, 59, 62, 85, 91
Triple Border, 40
True Scallop, 36, 46
Trumpet Vine, 97
Tulip, 116
Tuscan Shape, 35, 92
Twin Leaves, 42
Twisted Ribbon, 96

Union Shape, 18, 59, 63

Victor Shape, 34, 106, 107, 108
Victory, 116, 124
Vineyard, 126
Vintage Shape, 84, 130
Virginia Shape, 18, 63

Wall of Troy, 106
Washington Shape, 86, 92
Western Shape, 91, 100-101
Wheat, 69, 72, 73, 130, 135
Wheat and Blackberry, 71, 76, 135
Wheat and Clover, 23, 35, 71, 75
Wheat and Grape, 77
Wheat, Bulbous Shape, 72
Wheat in the Meadow, 77
Wheat with Flowers, 77
White Oak and Acorn, 80
Wild Rose Twig, 98
Winding Vine, 78
Winterberry, 85
Wrapped Sydenham, 56

## Handy Reference Pages

List of Staffordshire potters of ironstone, 27-30
List of American potters of ironstone, 138-140
Registration tables, 22-23
Cleaning directions, 141-144

# About the Author

Jean Wetherbee was born in Canajoharie (Indians called it, "the pot that washes itself") in the scenic Mohawk Valley of New York. Later, she and her husband Bernard reared four children on the six-generation family farm in that historic area. They declared, "A farm is the best place on earth to raise a family." Her love of the earth, joy in growing things, and interests in the past are reflected in her writings.

A former teacher and reading specialist, her interest in white ironstone evolved from her own collecting and curiosity about the origin of this hardy ware. Facts gathered in research were compiled in *A Handbook on White Ironstone* (1974).

Her newest book *A Look at White Ironstone,* is the product of ten years' study and travel in unearthing new data.

Presently, the Wetherbees make their home in Lynnfield, Massachusetts.